Praise for *10 Golden Stars to Leadership E*

"Finally, the perfect balance of theory and practice! Dr. Tom Dreyer has authored the only leadership book you'll ever need. Truly a masterpiece resource for every leader from the frontline to the C-Suite."
– Scott Jeffrey Miller
Bestselling author and Executive Vice-President, FranklinCovey; host of the world's largest leadership podcast

"The '10 Golden Stars' delivers neuroscientific insights and real-world wisdom, enabling leaders to transform today's challenges into opportunities with grace and effectiveness. It is a testament to innovative thinking, unlocking team potential and achieving lasting organizational success."
– Amna Al Mahri
Advisor to His Excellency Dr. Yasir Al Naqbi, Director General in the Abu Dhabi Department of Government Enablement

"As Dr. Tom Dreyer says, 'leadership is multidimensional and complex' and likely to get more challenging. The '10 Golden Stars' offers a rare blend of sharp insights, neuroscientific research, and practical tools, enabling modern leaders to better understand their roles. It also equips them to uplift the performance of their teams."
– Richard Hargreaves
Managing Director, Corporate Research Forum

"Tom has achieved something remarkable here, bringing in-depth research and decades of experience into this valuable resource, which is empowering and enlightening. It's often uncomfortable to hold up the mirror and self-reflect, but these stars ease the process and guide your every step. Simply a must-have toolkit for navigating the complexities of modern leadership."
– Yousef Bin Mohamed
CEO, Taaeen Consulting and Talent Development

"The layout and content are exceptionally user-friendly, and applicable to all levels from aspiring leaders to seasoned executives and HC professionals who are on a self-awareness and development journey. It offers practical tools and real-life success stories for meaningful reflection on leadership practices. The emphasis on neuroscience stands out, providing key insights into human behavior. It's a comprehensive guide for navigating leadership in our interconnected world."
– Prof Deseré Kokt
Professor of Human Resource Management, Central University of Technology

"It is like finding a treasure chest in the leadership world, a journey that helps you look at leadership with fresh eyes and wit. This book doesn't just tell you to be better; it shows you how, all while keeping it light-hearted and real. Get ready to be inspired and shake up your leadership approach."

– Saeed Al Shamisi
Group Chief Human Capital Officer, Abu Dhabi National Exhibition Centre (ADNEC)

"The *10 Golden Stars of Leadership Excellence* by Dr. Tom Dreyer is an impactful yet straightforward guide for modern leaders. By weaving real-life examples with leadership theories, this book bridges the gap between theory and practice. It's not just a one-time read, it's a companion for your growth journey. Carry it with you, like a trusted mentor!"

– Jozsef Blasko
Senior Vice-president, Human Resources, TAQA

"The '10 Golden Stars' cuts through the noise with sharp insights and no-nonsense strategies for today's leaders. Dr. Tom Dreyer gets what modern leadership is all about and makes it easy to up your game. A keeper on your desk; it's the kind of book you'll want all your leaders and peers to read."

– Jason English
Author, Speaker, and CEO of CG Tech Group

YOUR ULTIMATE GUIDE

10

GOLDEN STARS

TO

LEADERSHIP
EXCELLENCE

Accelerate your leadership development with modern
theory and practice to build high-performance teams

DR. TOM DREYER

Quickfox

Published by Quickfox Publishing
Cape Town, South Africa
www.quickfox.co.za | info@quickfox.co.za

10 Golden Stars to Leadership Excellence
ISBN paperback: 978-0-7961-5043-1
ISBN ePub: 978-0-7961-5044-8
ISBN Kindle: 978-0-7961-5939-7
ISBN audiobook: 978-0-7961-5045-5

First edition 2024

Edited by Gill Gordon
Cover concept by Poli Dreyer

For special orders, bulk sales, corporate sales, trade and wholesale sales,
and course adoptions, please email leadership@drtomdreyer.com

Dedicated to all present and future leaders
who strive to lead with purpose,
learn with passion, and shape a legacy.
May these Golden Stars illuminate
your journey to leadership excellence.

Lead with purpose.
Learn with passion.
Shape a legacy.

CONTENTS

GOLDEN STAR 5 DEVELOPING HIGH-PERFORMANCE TEAMS 117

GOLDEN STAR 6 THE POWER OF EI AND NLP 143

GOLDEN STAR 9 LEADING IN THE DIGITAL AGE....... 213

GOLDEN STAR 10 TALENT DEVELOPMENT 229

BONUS STARS

Epilogue

Before you begin, scan the QR code to redeem your
complimentary digital tools, or download them from:

drtomdreyer.com/tools

INTRODUCTION

Congratulations on taking this powerful first step! You have already demonstrated the curiosity, passion for learning, and quest for growth that are essential for every successful leader. By taking a journey through the *10 Golden Stars to Leadership Excellence*, you are following a path that is educational, inspirational, and deeply insightful. This book will challenge you, uplift you, encourage you, and ultimately transform you into a leader of substance and stature.

Being a leader of people is a role filled with complexities, obstacles, and sacrifices. A well-equipped leader, armed with the right mental attitude, necessary skills, and practical tools, not only thrives, but also finds profound fulfillment in leading an engaged and motivated team.

My journey to leadership has been deeply rewarding, igniting a passion to inspire leaders to lead with purpose, learn with passion, and shape a legacy. I've had the privilege to partner with leading institutions such as Harvard, London Business School, Central University of Technology, Franklin Covey, and many more, while spearheading leadership development teams, projects, and programs in major global organizations. This has allowed me to directly empower over 4000 leaders from 119 different nationalities with practical insights and transformative tools. Along this journey, I've navigated numerous leadership challenges and learned invaluable lessons, all of which I'm eager to share with you.

In these pages, I distill over 20 years of experience, insights from a global network of leadership development experts, neuroscientists, academics, and renowned leaders. But *10 Golden Stars to Leadership Excellence* isn't about me; it is about encouraging you to discover what works for you on your own leadership journey. Through self-reflection, and the application of new skills, this book will give you the tools you need to convert obstacles into opportunities for success.

10 Golden Stars to success

As part of my doctoral research, I studied the obstacles that leaders commonly face, and how to overcome them. I analyzed best practices, and looked at how neuroscience contributes towards successful outcomes. This inspired me to establish the "10 Golden Stars", the bedrock of my leadership philosophy. By applying these insights to your own leadership practice, you'll learn how to overcome challenges, and set yourself on an accelerated path to leadership excellence.

Golden Star 1: Growing your leadership self-awareness

"Good leadership begins with an inward journey."

The ancient Greeks had a saying, "Know thyself", which is as relevant for modern leaders as it was centuries ago. Lack of self-awareness occurs when leaders lose touch with their personal strengths, weaknesses, emotions, and core values. They may struggle to foster trust and authenticity, be overwhelmed by their perceived shortcomings, and fail to make the most of their strengths. This sets up a disconnect that can skew decision-making, dampen team morale, and hinder their ability to adapt to changing environments.

Neuroscience links self-awareness to neuroplasticity (the brain's capacity to forge neural connections). Addressing a lack of self-awareness requires a willingness to accept honest feedback. You also need to undertake a measure of self-reflection, not just to identify areas for personal development, but to recognize and utilize your inherent strengths. Adaptability enables leaders to better understand and manage their emotions and behaviors. Improved emotional intelligence, grounded in the brain's limbic system, is a direct outcome of heightened self-awareness, which is crucial for empathic and effective leadership[1].

Golden Star 1 explains the difference between leading and managing, and explores how different aspects of leadership can align with your personal values. You will discover how to nurture a growth mindset, and cultivate learning agility.

Being self-aware fosters a deeper sense of who we are. This, in turn, enhances authenticity, strengthens relationships, and helps build cohesive teams. Knowing yourself will sharpen your decision-making, improve personal communications, and establish a solid base on which to build your leadership practice. Self-awareness, the foundation of transformative leadership, not only marks the beginning of a journey towards success, it promotes true excellence in leadership.

Golden Star 2: Discovering your leadership style

"Effective leadership flows like water, adapting its form in response to each situation."

A rigid leadership style occurs when leaders adhere to one approach, regardless of the prevailing situation or interpersonal dynamics. Rigid leaders often become less effective. They may struggle to connect with their teams, and their unbending approach can stifle growth and creativity. In a dynamic business environment, this can quickly become counterproductive. An inability to adapt to change can suppress team potential and innovation, resulting in a stagnant work culture.

Overcoming rigidity begins with recognizing that no single approach fits every situation or circumstance. Situational leadership is about recognizing and responding to specific situations, embracing diversity within teams, and fostering an environment of respect and growth. A flexible approach allows you to lead with agility, and adapt to changing contexts.

Golden Star 2 explores how leaders can identify their unique style, and adjust it according to what their team needs at the time. Shifting from a rigid style to a more flexible approach is the basis for establishing a personal leadership style that is dynamic, empathic, and responsive.

Golden Star 3: Understanding your team

"Teams are like a puzzle. When all the pieces fit together,
you see the whole picture."

Even the most competent leaders can misunderstand team dynamics. They fail to acknowledge diverse personalities, generational differences, or individual motivations. Leaders who misread interpersonal dynamics might experience breakdowns in communication, or lower levels of collaboration, and struggle to motivate their team effectively. A misalignment between the leader's approach and the team's potential is like trying to fit a square peg into a round hole, and this can result in an environment where talent is underutilized, and team cohesion is weakened.

Golden Star 3 looks at the challenge of assimilating different personalities and ages into an effective team. It examines various models for assessing personality, and understanding behavior, and provides strategies on how to integrate the diversity of values and perspectives that can occur in multi-generational teams.

Being willing to accommodate differences fosters an environment where every individual's potential is maximized, and facilitates the creation of a harmonious and dynamic team. A willingness to recognize diverse talents can also be leveraged for greater success.

Understanding team dynamics will transform how leaders truly connect with their team. When individual preferences, strengths, and motivations align with the team's goals, the result is improved communication, increased collaboration, better relationships, and a more cohesive team. Golden Star 3 is about unlocking the potential of diverse teams, and paving the way for a leadership journey that is as rewarding as it is successful.

Golden Star 4: Building trust

"Trust is the silent heartbeat of effective leadership."

Lack of trust develops when a leader loses confidence in their team, or a team loses confidence in their leader. Erosion of trust typically stems from lack of transparency, unfulfilled promises, or inconsistencies in attitude or approach. It stifles innovation, reduces willingness to take risks or support others, and inhibits the free exchange of ideas.

Golden Star 4 emphasizes the foundational role of trust in relationships, and explores avenues for developing it. Trust is more than a concept. It is a practice that propels teams towards unity, commitment, and impactful results. Establishing trust with others shapes the brain's responses, and has a positive influence on individual behaviors and attitudes. The Trust-to-Results pyramid is an effective technique for creating a culture where trust is nurtured and protected. As a leader, building, and maintaining, a bond of trust with your team will help you establish a bond of confidence and mutual respect.

Golden Star 5: Developing high-performance teams

"A successful team leader maximizes the potential of every member, and unites them behind a single idea or purpose."

Most leaders aspire to lead a high-performance team. However, many leaders find it challenging to meld individuals into a cohesive unit. This can result in a lack of synergy, and reduce collaboration, leading to underperformance and disengagement. Other consequences of ineffective team building are misaligned goals, indistinct roles, and a failure to leverage individual potential. Teams caught in this trap often exhibit low morale, decreased productivity, and a general sense of stagnation.

Golden Star 5 offers a roadmap for transforming a group of individuals into a unified team. It introduces models for assessing and developing high-performance teams, as well as models for fostering engagement, which is the emotional and intellectual commitment a person has towards their role.

Developing a high-performance team requires setting realistic goals, establishing clear roles, agreeing on a strategy, and then implementing it. This comprehensive approach will enable leaders to transform their teams into dynamic, effective units that can achieve outstanding results.

Golden Star 6: The power of emotional intelligence and NLP

"Leaders who sail the seas of emotions discover the treasure of deep connections."

Emotion is a powerful force. Leaders who fail to recognize this can experience a disconnect with their team members, reducing their ability to lead effectively. People who lack emotional intelligence (EI) may struggle to forge meaningful connections with others. Overlooking communication cues can result in misunderstandings, and a disengaged workforce. Good leaders are able to connect with their team members on an individual level, emphasize interpersonal dynamics, and foster a spirit of collaboration. Neuroscience reveals that emotional regulation is critical for decision-making, relationship-building, and calculated risk-taking; all areas where leaders with high EI excel[2].

Golden Star 6 examines the role of emotions in the workplace. It guides leaders through the nuances of emotional intelligence, and the importance of empathy in effective leadership. It also explores neurolinguistic programming, with insights into how to use it to understand and influence team behavior. Harnessing the power of EI and neurolinguistic programming (NLP) can transform your leadership practice by helping you develop an empathic, engaged, and successful team.

Golden Star 7: Mastering communication

"Effective leaders know how to make their words count."

Mastering the skill of good communication is a leader's lifeline. The results of poor communication can be a cascade of misinterpretation, confusion, and misaligned efforts, which reach to the core of team dynamics. Unclear instructions can make it harder to complete tasks, while a lack of empathy erodes the bedrock of trust and morale. Neuroscience reveals how effective communication resonates deeply with our brain's preference for clarity, empathy, and understanding[3].

Golden Star 7 explores listening and speaking, as well as the art of asking questions and telling stories. Good communication skills include listening carefully, speaking with clarity, and interpreting non-verbal cues. When your messages are not just conveyed, but are well received and fully understood, you will connect in a more meaningful way.

As a leader, your words have the power to influence, motivate, and inspire; but only if they are heard. This chapter introduces communication techniques that will foster understanding and interpersonal connection by means of practical and impactful models for active listening, effective questioning, giving feedback, and public speaking.

Golden Star 8: Resilience, adaptability, and transformation

"Adaptable leaders turn the winds of change into the energy that propels their team forward."

Most of us resist change, preferring to maintain the status quo. However, change is inevitable in business. It can be hard to adapt to altered circumstances and, more importantly, to lead your team through a period of change, but the cost of inflexibility is significant. In business, failure to transform can result in stagnation, missed opportunities, and an inability to fully develop your potential.

Golden Star 8 equips leaders to view change as an opportunity for growth, not a force to be resisted. Adapting to change is about developing a mindset where change is both anticipated and welcomed. Leaders who are resilient and forward-looking can confidently guide their teams through the complexities of change. This chapter explores what it means to be both resilient and adaptable, and gives leaders the tools to transform change into positive and dynamic growth.

Golden Star 9: Leading in the digital age

"Leaders must navigate the digital currents in order to
steer their teams into safe waters."

We live in a rapidly evolving digital world. Artificial intelligence (AI) is transforming business on every level, and doing so at a bewildering pace. Technological innovation has the power to drive change, accelerate innovation, and dramatically alter the workplace. The challenge is to recognize what works for you, and not get sidetracked by the hype over every new tool or model.

Golden Star 9 explores various aspects of the digital workspace, including the rise of remote work, and the ethical implications of AI. Digital transformation starts with the recognition that integrating new technology with existing practices and procedures is not just an operational necessity, it is a leadership imperative. Today's leaders must know how to harness the appropriate digital tools in ways that meet their team's strategic objectives, as well as enhance individual performance.

Having the confidence to embrace digital transformation will create opportunities for leaders to fast-track their team's growth and advancement.

Golden Star 10: Talent development

"Every interaction has the potential to influence, inspire, and motivate."

When people feel undervalued or underutilized, their motivation, performance levels, and ability to innovate decline. Part of a leader's role is to develop their team members to their fullest potential. By investing in and supporting individuals, leaders not only enhance their capabilities, but also establish a foundation for them to grow into future leaders, thereby sustaining the long-term success of the organization.

Golden Star 10 emphasizes the role that leaders play in unlocking individual potential. It guides leaders towards discovering their personal developer style, and introduces coaching and mentoring techniques infused with insights from neuroscience. The ability to delegate enables leaders to entrust team members with responsibilities that will expand their skills, while acknowledging improvements can encourage individuals to go further. Successful leaders nurture talent in others, and create an environment that inspires and motivates.

Mastering the 10 Golden Stars is not just about enhancing your personal leadership skill set. It is about making a profound impact on others, and sparking transformation in their lives, as well as enriching your own.

The journey has begun, so embrace a growth mindset and let the stars guide you towards your leadership goals. This is your moment to lead with purpose, learn with passion, and shape a legacy.

Endnotes

1   Lavrekhina, S. (2023). The Role of Neuroplasticity in Enhancing Leadership Skills. Neuroscience Business School.
     https://eunbs.com/the-role-of-neuroplasticity-in-enhancing-leadership-skills
2   Morawetz, C., Mohr, P. N. C., Heekeren, H. R., & Bode, S. (2019). The effect of emotion regulation on risk-taking and decision-related activity in the prefrontal cortex. *Social Cognitive and Affective Neuroscience*, 14(10), 1109–1118. https://doi.org/10.1093/scan/nsz078
3   Trevick, S., Kim, M., & Naidech, A. (2016). Communication, leadership, and decision-making in the Neuro-ICU. *Current Neurology and Neuroscience Reports*, 16(11), 99. https://doi.org/10.1007/s11910-016-0699-5

GOLDEN STAR

GROWING YOUR LEADERSHIP SELF-AWARENESS

Let's start our leadership journey by exploring two stories involving two very different men, in very different situations, who are often used as stellar examples of great leaders. The first is Anglo-Irish explorer Ernest Shackleton (1874–1922) who, in 1914, set out with 27 men on a mission to cross Antarctica. Their ship *Endurance* was crushed by pack ice, leaving the men stranded, with little hope of survival. What followed was a testament to incredible leadership. Despite their dire situation, Shackleton kept his crew's morale high, managed limited resources, made difficult decisions, and ultimately led his men to safety after a grueling two-year ordeal. Shackleton didn't have an MBA, but he understood the essence of leadership. It was not about giving orders or managing tasks. It was about taking care of his people, providing direction in a crisis, and leading by example.

The second story is about South Africa's Nelson Mandela (1918–2013). Jailed in 1962 for fighting for the rights of the Black majority, Mandela spent the next 27 years in a prison cell, only to emerge without bitterness, but with a will to reconcile a nation divided by the deep wounds of apartheid. Mandela's leadership was not characterized by highfalutin strategies or complex tactics, but by simple human values: forgiveness, humility, and an unwavering commitment to justice. His life serves as a shining beacon that illuminates our understanding of great leadership.

> Understanding the essence of leadership is the key to unlocking a multitude of benefits.

Seventy-five years separate the defining moments of these two men, yet their approach to leadership remains as relevant today as it was in their time. Regardless of the challenges that leaders face, they need to be flexible yet focused, powerful yet accountable, tech-savvy yet people-centered.

Understanding the essence of leadership is the key to unlocking a multitude of benefits for your personal development. It paves the way for better decision-making, enhanced emotional intelligence, and more authentic leadership. It equips you to lead with purpose and clarity, like a maestro conducting a symphony, ensuring that each note, each instrument, creates a harmony that resonates with success.

Leadership is not management

The road to discovering the essence of leadership is riddled with pitfalls and obstacles. One of the most prevalent missteps lies in the conflation of 'leadership' with 'management'. These terms are often used interchangeably, yet they are as distinct as the heart is from the brain. Leadership and management are vital organs in the body of an organization, and each serves an indispensable role, although their functions are fundamentally different.

> Leadership and management are vital organs in the body of an organization, and each serves an indispensable role, although their functions are fundamentally different.

I like to think of management as the brain, the organ that keeps the body functioning on a basic level. Management is about optimization, efficiency, and ensuring that day-to-day operations can proceed without a hitch. In management, the focus is on tasks, metrics, and the procedural functions of an organization. Managers aim to do things right. By following established guidelines, protocols, and performance indicators, they maintain the systems and structures that keep an organization stable. They are the stewards of routine, precision, and reliability.

Leadership, on the other hand, is like the heart, pumping energy and direction into an organization's veins. Leadership transcends the transactional elements of task completion and operational efficiency. It is about vision, transformation, and inspiring others towards a common goal. Leadership seeks to do the right things, which may not always be captured by current metrics or standard procedures. Leaders are like trailblazers or explorers. They carve out new pathways, challenge the status quo, and drive change. They cultivate a sense of purpose and inspire a culture of belonging among their team members.

It's essential to note that while all leaders may manage, not all managers necessarily lead. Leadership is less a of job description and more a vocation or a calling. It is an impulse to inspire, to influence, and to leave an indelible impact. Whereas management is concerned with the "how" and the "what", leadership is preoccupied with the "why" and the "what could be".

Leadership and management are both vital, but each serves a different, albeit complementary, role in an organization's health and success. Understanding this distinction is crucial for any aspiring leader who needs to navigate an intricate maze of responsibilities and challenges.

The multiple facets of leadership

Shackleton and Mandela were unique men, with distinct personalities, characteristics, values, strengths and weaknesses. Their individual characters and inherent strengths, coupled with what they experienced and endured in their lives, made them the ideal leaders for the situation they were facing. This holds true for any leader.

Another example of someone who was defined by their unique experience is Viktor Frankl (1905–1997), a Holocaust survivor who emerged from the concentration camps as a great teacher of resilience, and whose wisdom guides us to this day. Similarly, American abolitionist and social activist Harriet Tubman (1822–1913) escaped slavery herself before going on to establish a network of antislavery activists and safe houses, known as the Underground Railroad, that enabled former slaves to reach freedom.

Leadership is multidimensional and complex. One step in our understanding of leadership is acknowledging the perspectives of others who have helped to shape the field.

1. *Leadership is influence; nothing more, nothing less.* **John C. Maxwell,** leadership expert and author, emphasizes the critical aspect of influencing others towards a common goal.
2. *Leadership is the capacity to translate vision into reality.* **Warren Bennis,** scholar, organizational consultant, and author, underscores the ability to materialize a vision, an essential quality of effective leaders.

3. *As we look ahead into the next century, leaders will be those who empower others.* **Bill Gates**, co-founder of Microsoft, stresses the importance of empowerment in the context of future leadership.

4. *The function of leadership is to produce more leaders, not more followers.* **Ralph Nader**, political activist, views leadership as a catalyst for producing more leaders.

5. *Management is doing things right; leadership is doing the right things.* **Peter F. Drucker**, management consultant, educator, and author, distinguishes leadership from management by its focus on doing the right things.

6. *Leadership is unlocking people's potential to become better.* **Bill Bradley**, former U.S. Senator, and Hall of Fame basketball player, spotlights the role of a leader in enhancing individual potential.

7. *The greatest leader is not necessarily the one who does the greatest things. He is the one who gets people to do the greatest things.* **Ronald Reagan**, 40th President of the USA, emphasizes the leader's role in motivating and encouraging others to achieve greatness.

8. *Leadership is the art of getting someone else to do something you want done because he wants to do it.* **Dwight D. Eisenhower**, 34th President of the USA, depicts leadership as the art of inspiring willingness in others.

9. *Leadership is an action, not a position.* **Donald McGannon**, television broadcasting pioneer, underscores that leadership is about what you do, not the title you hold.

10. *A leader is one who knows the way, goes the way, and shows the way.* **John C. Maxwell** once again provides a definition that emphasizes the role model aspect of leadership.

These definitions, while varied, touch on different aspects of what makes a leader: influence, vision, empowerment, mentorship, integrity, fostering potential, inspiring greatness, cultivating willingness, taking action, and being a role model. Each definition offers a unique perspective, reflecting the diversity and depth of leadership as a concept.

It is important to remember that there isn't a single definition of leadership, and that there are no absolute rights or wrongs. The essence of business leadership can vary across countries, cultures, industries, and individual perspectives. It is a broad, flexible concept that can adapt to different scenarios and needs. The key is to absorb the insights of this Golden Star (and the others that follow), refine your understanding, and define what leadership means to *you* in your unique journey.

Discovering your personal leadership values

Exploring the concept of leadership calls for self-reflection and introspection. You need to understand the guiding principles, or values, that shape your leadership philosophy and influence the way you interact with others, make decisions, and respond to challenges.

Neuroscience adds another dimension to leadership development.[1] The human brain is highly plastic; that is, capable of change and adaptation. This neural plasticity allows us to learn from experiences, adapt to new circumstances, and even reshape our values over time.

> ... as we learn from our mistakes, or adapt to new challenges, the brain's neuroplasticity allows us to alter our leadership style accordingly.

Our brains tend to reinforce neural pathways that are linked to our habitual behaviors and thoughts. These well-trodden paths often reflect our current values and leadership style. However, when we take the time to consciously reflect on our values and leadership approach, we activate different parts of our brain, specifically the prefrontal cortex, which is the area responsible for complex cognitive behavior, decision-making, and moderating social behavior. This activation allows for the possibility of further change and adaptation.

New neural connections form as we challenge our current beliefs and values, or consider new perspectives. For instance, as we learn from our mistakes, or adapt to new challenges, the brain's neuroplasticity allows us to alter our leadership style accordingly. So, in a real sense, the journey of leadership evolution is not only metaphorical but also actual; it happens in our physical brains, as well as in our minds.

Reflecting on your leadership values is not a one-off event. Instead, a continuous process of neural rewiring enables self-discovery and growth. Your brain's marvellous ability to adapt and learn means that, as a leader, you're not static; rather, you are continually evolving. This understanding lends even more weight to the importance of conscious reflection and continual learning in leadership development.

Use these questions to explore what leadership means and clarify your leadership values:

1. **How do you define leadership?** When you think about what leadership means to you, what words or phrases come to mind?
2. **What qualities do you believe a good leader should possess?** Reflect on the traits and characteristics that you admire in other leaders. These might be qualities such as empathy, resilience, or strategic thinking.
3. **What is your leadership philosophy?** Your thoughts on what leadership means will inform your fundamental approach to leadership, and how you intend to lead others.
4. **What are your core leadership values?** The principles that guide your leadership approach might include values such as integrity, innovation, or inclusivity.
5. **Do your personal values align with your leadership values?** Reflect on how your personal values inform your leadership, and how they might influence your actions and decisions as a leader.
6. **Which leaders inspire you, and why?** Think about the leaders you admire, in your personal life, your career, or the public sphere. Which of their qualities or actions inspire you?
7. **How do you want to be perceived as a leader?** Consider how you would like others to view you. Does this align with your current leadership style and actions?
8. **What does success look like to you?** What do you want to achieve as a leader? This might include specific goals, or more abstract concepts, such as uplifting or empowering others, or driving innovation.
9. **Can you handle failure or setbacks?** Think about how you react when things don't go as planned. The way you deal with setbacks can reveal a lot about your resilience and adaptability.

10. **Do you inspire and motivate others?** Reflect on the strategies you use to encourage your team. How effective have these strategies been?

> Just as our body cannot function without a beating heart, organizations cannot thrive without effective leadership.

Remember, there are no right or wrong answers. The goal is to encourage introspection and self-awareness. As you continue along your leadership journey, you may want to revisit these questions from time to time, reflecting on how your views and approaches have evolved. Keep in mind that leadership is not about being the best; it focuses on making everyone else better.

But why is it necessary to understand the "anatomy" of leadership? Consider this: Leadership is the lifeblood of any organization, from global conglomerates to start-ups and non-profits. Just as our body cannot function without a beating heart, organizations cannot thrive without effective leadership. It drives performance, shapes culture, and influences everyone at every level. In a world that is constantly changing, leadership is the compass that guides us through uncertainty, enabling us to cope with challenges and disruption, and arrive at success by learning from previous pitfalls or setbacks.

A journey of learning

Leadership is a continuous journey of learning and evolving. To sustain a development mindset, leaders must:

1. **Assess and reflect** Regularly assess your leadership performance and practices. Reflect on the feedback you receive from team members, peers, and mentors. Consider what works and what doesn't work, and identify areas for improvement.
2. **Stay curious** Be open to new ideas, perspectives, and approaches. Expand your knowledge by reading widely, attending workshops and training sessions (in-person or online), and actively participating in group and one-on-one discussions.

3. **Be able to adapt** As a leader, the ability to adapt is invaluable. In an evolving business environment, your leadership approach should be flexible enough to adjust to changing circumstances, varying team needs, and organizational goals.

4. **Stay resilient** Not all your leadership practices will yield immediate results. Resilience helps you overcome setbacks and learn from the experience. It fuels your growth as a leader.

5. **Foster collaboration** Collaborative environments help to promote continuous learning and development. Encourage diverse points of view and foster a culture of open dialogue and shared decision-making.

6. **Practice empathy** Empathy strengthens personal connections, builds trust, and promotes a supportive work culture. As you develop your leadership skills, always keep empathy at the forefront.

7. **Commit to lifelong learning** Make learning a priority. Set personal development goals, engage in self-directed learning, and keep expanding your knowledge and business-related skills.

Nurturing your growth mindset

On our leadership voyage, it is easy to get so caught up in developing others that we neglect our own growth, but a stagnant leader cannot drive a dynamic team. The concept of the "growth mindset", developed by American psychologist Carol Dweck, is critical for leadership success. A growth mindset is about deeply understanding and truly believing that our talents and abilities can be developed and shaped by dedication, hard work, and a love of learning. It is recognizing that failures or setbacks are merely detours on the path to success.

But how do we translate a growth mindset into real-life actions? How can you, as a leader, ensure you are continuously growing and becoming

A growth mindset is about deeply understanding and truly believing that our talents and abilities can be developed and shaped by dedication, hard work, and a love of learning.

better every day? This is where a personal development plan comes into play.

Creating a personal development plan is not about rigidly scheduling every minute of your day, nor is it about setting lofty, unattainable goals. It is about creating a roadmap to your personal self-improvement, starting with identifying where you are now, where you want to be, and how you are going to get there. It's about setting SMART goals (Specific, Measurable, Achievable, Relevant, Time-bound) that will stretch you, but that will still be within your reach, keeping yourself accountable, and tracking your progress to ensure continuous growth.

A practical way to start your personal development plan is to conduct a SWOT analysis (Strengths, Weaknesses, Opportunities, Threats) on yourself. This will allow you to assess your current capabilities, identify areas where you feel you need to improve, and outline strategies for how to achieve your goals. This book provides you with plenty of self-reflection pit stops, so make use of them.

> Self-directed learning is about taking ownership of your own learning journey. Instead of waiting for someone else to tell you how to improve, take the initiative to identify, pursue, and evaluate your learning options.

Just creating a plan isn't enough, though. What is even more critical is the implementation, and this is where self-directed learning comes in. Self-directed learning is about taking ownership of your own learning journey. Instead of waiting for someone else to tell you how to improve, take the initiative to identify, pursue, and evaluate your learning options. Become proactive rather than reactive. Acquire the knowledge and skills you need; don't wait for them to be handed to you.

Directing your own learning journey doesn't mean you have to do it alone. Seek advice and guidance, ask for feedback, and collaborate with others. Remember, you are the one driving your growth. When you take control, you'll find that learning becomes a passion, not a chore. You will be learning because you *want* to, not because you *have* to.

In your day-to-day work life, it is easy to become weighed down with management responsibilities and to ignore your own needs, but taking care of your personal development and growth as a leader is as much your responsibility as leading your team. As the saying goes, you cannot pour from an empty cup.

Harnessing resources for continuous development

Your development journey doesn't have to be solitary. Look around, and you will find people who are willing to offer insight, experience, and lessons. When it comes to training, mentoring, and networking opportunities, we have a wealth of resources at our fingertips. Leadership programs, workshops, webinars, online courses, and books are just a few clicks away. They present a variety of perspectives and techniques that will enhance your skills, deepen your knowledge, and keep you up-to-date with the latest trends and practices.

> Your development journey doesn't have to be solitary. Look around, and you will find people who are willing to offer insight, experience, and lessons.

Mentoring can be a profound catalyst for growth. Whether it's a formal program or an informal mentor-mentee relationship, having a personal mentor who can provide valuable feedback and guidance will accelerate your development. You can even have multiple mentors who provide different perspectives, and lessons based on their experiences.

Networking, or building relationships, with fellow leaders, colleagues, and subordinates, can unlock countless learning opportunities, from comparing best practices to sharing thought-provoking insights. Don't be afraid to attend a networking event, initiate a conversation, ask a question, or discuss an experience. You never know what gems of wisdom you might stumble upon in the process.

Learning opportunities also come from our day-to-day experiences. Success and setbacks are potent teachers. They provide us with real-time, context-specific lessons that no book or course can match. To extract these lessons, we need to adopt a reflective mindset, and analyze our experiences to understand what worked, what didn't, and why. This isn't about dwelling on the past, it is about learning from it to create a better future.

Feedback, especially constructive criticism, is not always easy to accept, but it is crucial for growth. It holds up a mirror to our actions, attitudes, and the impact we make, revealing our blind spots and areas for improvement. It also highlights strengths. Seek feedback from your peers, your team, your mentors, and even yourself. Embrace it, learn from it, and use it to become a better version of yourself as a leader.

Maxwell's 5 Levels of Leadership

Development isn't a linear process; it's more akin to a ladder where each step represents a distinct phase of growth. John C. Maxwell, renowned leadership expert, encapsulates this in his 5 Levels of Leadership, which outlines the journey a leader takes, identifies your current level, and provides steps to maximize your personal potential.

LEVEL 1 **Position: Leadership by title** People follow you because they *have* to, not because they *want* to. Your influence comes solely from your job title. This might seem like a great place to start, but if you rely solely on positional authority, your leadership growth will be stunted. To be an effective leader, you need to build relationships and show your team that you value them.

LEVEL 2 **Permission: Leadership by relationship** People follow you because they *want* to. You build strong relationships by treating your team members with respect, trust, and appreciation. This approach will enable you to inspire and influence them more effectively. At Level 2, people will begin to follow you based on how you treat them, and not just because of your positional power.

LEVEL 3 **Production: Leadership by results** People follow you because of what you have done for the organization. You've demonstrated your competence, and your team's morale is high. As you work collaboratively to achieve common goals, you gain credibility as a leader, and create momentum that drives the organization forward.

LEVEL 4 **People development: Leadership by reproduction** People follow you because of what you have done for them personally. At this level, you don't just achieve organizational goals, you help others to achieve their own goals, and become leaders themselves. By mentoring, training, and developing your team members, you multiply your own influence.

LEVEL 5 **Pinnacle: Leadership by respect** People follow you because of who you are, and what you represent. Your reputation for excellence and integrity ensures that your influence extends beyond your immediate sphere. Pinnacle leaders foster leadership in others, and create a legacy of leadership in their organization.

MAXWELL'S 5 LEVELS OF LEADERSHIP

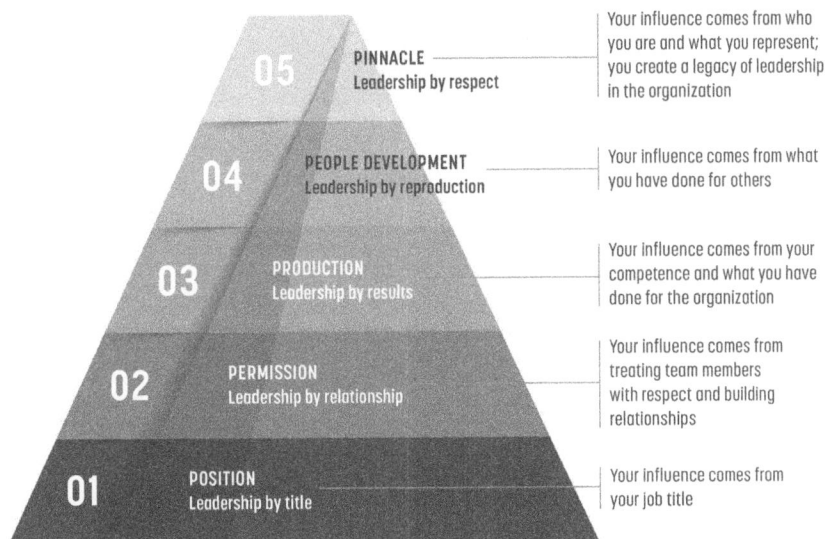

05 PINNACLE
Leadership by respect — Your influence comes from who you are and what you represent; you create a legacy of leadership in the organization

04 PEOPLE DEVELOPMENT
Leadership by reproduction — Your influence comes from what you have done for others

03 PRODUCTION
Leadership by results — Your influence comes from your competence and what you have done for the organization

02 PERMISSION
Leadership by relationship — Your influence comes from treating team members with respect and building relationships

01 POSITION
Leadership by title — Your influence comes from your job title

The 5 Levels of Leadership offer a clear pathway for personal development, but progressing through them takes time and dedication. Maxwell emphasizes that each level serves as a foundation for the next, and leaders should continually strive to improve themselves, and climb to the next level. By understanding the 5 Levels, leaders can recognize their current level and develop plans to make a more significant impact on their team and organization.

As you reflect on these levels, consider the following questions:

- Which level of leadership do you believe you've achieved?
- What actions can you take to get to the next level?
- How does your current leadership level affect both your team and your organization?
- Will applying these levels help you to develop other leaders?

Understanding and applying Maxwell's 5 Levels of Leadership can help you grow as a leader, and illuminate the path ahead.

Cultivating learning agility: Thriving in the face of change

Learning agility is the ability to learn, unlearn, and relearn quickly, allowing us to adapt and thrive in fast-changing environments. It is about shifting gears, adjusting focus, and being comfortable with the uncomfortable. Fast-paced, ever-evolving business landscapes demand agility from us. But how do we cultivate it?

> When you are faced with disruption, instead of retreating, lean in, observe, reflect, and learn.

The first step is to regard change and disruption as learning opportunities, not threats. It is during periods of intense change that we are pushed out of our comfort zones, and challenged to stretch, adapt, and innovate. Just as a diamond is formed under extreme pressure, our true potential unfolds during challenges and uncertainties. When you are faced with disruption, instead of retreating, lean in, observe, reflect, and learn. Every change brings a lesson, and every disruption is an opportunity for growth.

Comfort zones are, well ... comfortable. But comfort can be the enemy of growth. To grow, we need to step into the unknown, push our boundaries, and stretch ourselves. The way to do this is by setting goals that lie beyond our current skills and knowledge, demand more from us, and compel us to learn, innovate, and improve. So set that audacious goal, and take on that difficult project. The path might be steep, but the view from the top, and the growth you will achieve, will be worth the climb.

Once you have set your goals, you need to take steps to make them happen. It's one thing to acquire knowledge and skills passively, but we need to apply them to real-world challenges. It is in the doing, the practical application, that abstract concepts transform into tangible competencies, and theoretical knowledge morphs into practical wisdom. Don't just learn, do! Experiment, implement, try, fail, learn, and try again.

Cultivating learning agility may seem daunting, but it is about progress, not perfection. It's about consistently stepping forward, no matter how small the steps might be. As you continue on your journey, always remember that you're not just a leader; you are also a learner, a seeker, an adventurer, ready to navigate into the unknown, to learn, grow, and become a beacon of inspiration for others.

STORY IN PRACTICE

Growing from rookie to top-notch leader

Elizabeth Johnson, an ambitious young professional in the finance sector, was eager to climb the corporate ladder. Having been recently promoted, she faced the challenge of leading a team for the first time. This was amplified by her diverse team comprising both long-term employees and relatively inexperienced new hires.

As a leader, Elizabeth had always been praised for her competence and reliability. Initially, her mindset did not change. She focused on the operational aspects of leadership, such as monitoring budgets, managing tasks, meeting deadlines, and streamlining her team's schedules to make them more efficient. Yet, something was wrong. From the start, she found the team demotivated and resistant. She wondered whether they were missing their former leader, and were perhaps resentful of a newcomer. But he had a reputation for being difficult to work for, frequently criticizing team members, and taking credit for their best work. Rumor had it that he was not missed at all. So, what could it be?

Suddenly, Elizabeth recognized the problem. It had nothing to do with the former team leader. Instead, it was about her leadership style. Although she was being a good manager, she was not being a good leader. She was managing processes when she should be motivating people. Elizabeth set out to define what leadership meant to her, and align her leadership values with her personal values. After she discovered Maxwell's 5 Levels of Leadership, she recognized that being an effective leader depends on the strength of the bonds you build with your team.

A naturally empathic person who believed in the power of collaboration and inclusive decision-making, she understood that leadership provides opportunities to guide and develop others, helping them grow.

Maxwell's Level 1 became the starting point on her leadership journey. Elizabeth began by connecting with each of her team members and letting them know that they were valued. Having made the decision to progress from one level to another, she moved on to Level 2, building relationships that are based on mutual respect, trust and appreciation. Once she accomplished this, morale improved, and her team became more willing to collaborate towards meeting Level 3, achieving common organizational goals. By Level 4, Elizabeth was acknowledging individual effort, and encouraging team members to achieve their personal goals. At each level, she worked hard to gain the approval of her team by being a better leader. By the time she reached Level 5, both she and her team members recognized the benefits of establishing a positive working environment.

The transformation in Elizabeth was noticeable, but so was the impact on her team members, who responded enthusiastically to a leader who was nurturing and supportive. The more harmonious work environment became a catalyst for renewed vigor, and productivity soon increased. Elizabeth's empathic and inclusive approach earned her the respect and admiration of not only her team but also her superiors.

As she continued to progress in her career, Elizabeth realized that her success as a leader wasn't measured just in meeting targets or achieving results, but in the personal growth and development of her team members. She took pride in them as individuals, and hoped that some of them would become future leaders themselves.

Elizabeth Johnson is a shining example of a leader who, despite her initial uncertainties, recognized that reflecting on her role, and cultivating sound habits, would not only develop her as a leader, but help her create a collaborative, motivated team. Her journey reminds us that leadership is a continuous process of learning, adapting, and growing, and that anyone who is committed can become a successful leader.

SELF-REFLECTION PIT STOP

Scan the QR code or visit drtomdreyer.com/tools to download your e-toolkit.

Leadership foundations

Use this pit stop to establish your leadership foundations, recognize your strengths, and identify areas for improvement. Regularly revisiting your goals and reflections will help you track your progress, and make the necessary adjustments to keep you moving forward.

Part 1: Define leadership

1. Compare your understanding of leadership with what has been covered in this Golden Star. Which aspects align, and are there areas where you need to evolve?
2. On which of the 5 Levels of Leadership would you place yourself? What behaviors or actions contribute to your self-assessment? Write down some specific examples.

Part 2: Align personal and professional values

1. Consider how your personal values align with your leadership practices and whether they could influence your decisions and actions as a leader.

2. Identify any instances where your actions as a leader might have conflicted with your personal values. What caused this misalignment, how did you address it, and what did you learn from the experience?

Part 3: Set SMART goals

Based on your reflections above, set two or three SMART goals to improve your leadership skills. Each goal should be directly related to the content of this Golden Star. For example, if you want to strengthen your Level 4 leadership (People development), a SMART goal might be: "Over the next six months, I will dedicate at least four hours per week to enhancing professional development opportunities for my team, encouraging or enabling them to attend webinars, read industry-related literature, or take relevant online courses."

Leadership is a journey, not a destination. It is an ongoing process of learning, growing, and evolving. Keep your mind open, your heart humble, and your spirit resilient.

Endnotes

1   O'Connell, B., Logan, G., & Beauchamp, M. H. (2019). The importance of neuroplasticity in the brain's response to rehabilitation and leadership development. *NeuroLeadership Journal*.
Wang, Y., & Li, S. (2021). Neural mechanisms of leadership decision-making: A resting-state fMRI study. *Frontiers in Psychology*, 12, 634827.
Edmondson, A. C., & Verdin, P. J. (2020). Learning from mistakes: Cognitive and neural patterns in adaptive leadership. *Leadership Quarterly*, 31(1), 101376.

STAR **1** GROWING YOUR LEADERSHIP
SELF-AWARENESS

STAR **2** DISCOVERING YOUR LEADERSHIP STYLE

STAR **3** UNDERSTANDING YOUR TEAM

STAR **4** BUILDING TRUST

STAR **5** DEVELOPING HIGH-PERFORMANCE TEAMS

STAR **6** THE POWER OF EI AND NLP

STAR **7** MASTERING COMMUNICATION

STAR **8** RESILIENCE, ADAPTABILITY AND
TRANSFORMATION

STAR **9** LEADING IN THE DIGITAL AGE

STAR **10** TALENT DEVELOPMENT

GOLDEN STAR

DISCOVERING YOUR LEADERSHIP STYLE

This Golden Star explores the concept of leadership styles and situational leadership. Every leader has a unique style that reflects their personality, experiences, and the context in which they operate, and which shapes their decision-making and personal interactions. You will learn how to identify your own leadership style, recognize its strengths and pitfalls, and understand how to refine it for maximum impact.

Leaders need to be adaptable and flexible. Varying situations or circumstances might necessitate a shift in your leadership style, but by recognizing the implications for your team and organization, you can seamlessly manage these shifts.

Whether you lean towards the collaborative decision-making of democratic leadership, or align more with autocratic leadership, believing that an effective leader is one who makes all the decisions, this Golden Star will serve as a mirror, reflecting back your leadership persona. As with any reflection, your style is not etched in stone, but rather is a fluid, dynamic entity, receptive to development and fine-tuning.

Neuroscience supplements our understanding here. According to research, our brains constantly reshape our neural pathways in response to new experiences, a phenomenon known as neuroplasticity.[1] In the context of leadership, neuroplasticity implies that your style is not fixed. Instead, it is something that can change and evolve as your brain responds to experiences, challenges, and feedback.

As you learn and grow, your brain builds new connections and strengthens existing ones, allowing you to adapt your leadership style in response to new insights.

Nine common leadership styles

Knowing your leadership style gives you the knowledge to offer appropriate guidance and feedback to your team. It enables you to decipher your decision-making process and understand how to craft strategies that dovetail with your leadership ethos. But, perhaps most crucially, it offers a peek into your team's perception of you, casting light on *their* feedback and concerns.

Imagine a situation where your team feels unable to voice their ideas, or constrained in their creativity. If their feedback suggests that you lean towards an autocratic style of leadership, recognizing this might be your first step towards moderating your approach.

Let's examine some of the most prevalent leadership styles.

1. Democratic leadership

Also known as participative or facilitative leadership, this approach fosters a sense of collaboration and joint decision-making. While the leader still has the final say, each team member is encouraged to share their perspective and contribute to the decision-making process. Democratic leadership can be time-consuming and challenging, particularly if some team members lack the capacity to contribute meaningfully to critical decisions.

2. Autocratic leadership

This is characterized by decisions being made solely by the leader, with little to no input from team members. Autocratic leaders often have a clear vision and can make quick decisions, which might be beneficial during a crisis, or if the team lacks experience, but this style can result in a lack of creativity and employee dissatisfaction, particularly when decisions are made without consultation, or consideration for their impact on the team.

3. Laissez-faire leadership

Laissez-faire, or hands-off, leadership gives team members significant autonomy, with minimal intervention by the leader. This promotes a relaxed work culture and can spark creativity, particularly in skilled teams. However, it may be challenging for inexperienced teams, resulting in a sense of disconnection or detachment, where team cohesion and collaboration diminish because of the lack of active guidance and structured support from the leader.

4. Transformational leadership

Transformational leaders motivate and inspire their teams to exceed expectations, fostering personal growth and development. This style can encourage innovative thinking and improve morale and productivity.

Transformational leaders are good at encouraging and directing individual learning curves, but at the same time, they must ensure their quest for advancement does not result in employee burnout.

5. Coaching leadership

Leaders who coach focus on nurturing individual strengths and fostering team collaboration. They actively support skills development and independent problem-solving. However, this approach can be time-consuming, and not every employee responds well to coaching.

6. Bureaucratic leadership

Bureaucratic leaders strictly adhere to rules and procedures. While this can provide job security and predictability, it can stifle innovation and limit flexibility, making it less suitable for companies seeking rapid growth or creative solutions.

7. Transactional leadership

Transactional leadership is reward-based, offering incentives for meeting specific goals. While this style can provide clear expectations and rewards, it can also limit creativity and engagement, particularly if team members are not motivated by rewards alone.

8. Visionary leadership

Visionary leaders are future-oriented, inspiring their teams toward long-term goals. They are effective communicators who can foresee, and plan for, potential challenges. However, they often overlook day-to-day issues, or become too focused on a single goal.

9. Pacesetting leadership

Pacesetters set high expectations and standards for themselves, and demand the same level of commitment and performance from their teams. This can motivate skilled teams, but can lead to stress and burnout if goals are perceived as unrealistic or unattainable.

Situational leadership

Situational leadership calls for a shift in leadership style based on the circumstances at any given time. It embraces the dynamic nature of leadership and promotes understanding between leaders and their teams. The concept, which was first introduced by Paul Hersey and Ken Blanchard in the late 1960s, is based on the premise that no single "best" style of leadership fits all situations. Instead, successful leadership is determined by assessing the specific task at hand and adapting your style accordingly. The key to situational leadership is recognizing that different situations require different leadership approaches.

The key to situational leadership is recognizing that different situations require different leadership approaches.

Situational leadership calls for adaptability and flexibility on the part of the leader, an understanding of team dynamics, as well as knowing the strengths and weaknesses of team members. It begins with an assessment of the "maturity level" of the individuals in your team. This is not about age or experience, it refers to competence (ability, skills, knowledge) and commitment (confidence, motivation, willingness). Understanding each team member's maturity level (M1–M4) allows you to determine how much direction or support they need.

Situational leadership divides maturity levels into four broad categories:

1. **Low Competence, Low Commitment (M1):** Team members are new, inexperienced, possibly insecure, or unwilling to take responsibility.
2. **Low Competence, High Commitment (M2):** Individuals lack specific skills, but they are enthusiastic and committed.
3. **High Competence, Variable Commitment (M3):** Team members are generally capable, but they may lack the confidence or willingness to undertake tasks independently.
4. **High Competence, High Commitment (M4):** Individuals are experienced, skilled, and tend to be confident in their ability to handle tasks autonomously.

Four Approaches to situational leadership

The Four Approaches model considers individual levels of maturity (measured by competence and commitment) in team members. Each approach can be effective, depending on the situation.

Approach 1: Telling, directing, and guiding

This approach is particularly effective when dealing with team members who have low levels of competence and commitment (M1), indicated by their lack of knowledge, skills, and/or the experience necessary to successfully complete the tasks at hand.

1. **One-way communication** The leader makes all the decisions, telling team members what to do, and giving explicit instructions on how to do it. Team members have little input.
2. **The leader as "director"** The leader directs the process by providing step-by-step guidance. They set clear expectations and follow through with a high level of supervision that ensures tasks are carried out correctly and efficiently, as directed.
3. **High-directive behavior** Leaders give specific instructions, but then encourage team members to get on with the tasks, guiding them only when necessary. They monitor performance closely to minimize errors and ensure precise execution of tasks.

> Telling, directing, and guiding works best in situations where margins for error are low, and the cost of mistakes is high.

Telling, directing, and guiding works best in situations where margins for error are low, and the cost of mistakes is high. It helps bridge the knowledge and experience gap for M1 (low maturity) individuals by fostering an environment where they can build their competence and confidence, and reassuring them that guidance is readily available as they navigate new challenges. It is also beneficial when new tasks or projects are introduced, and team members have yet to acquire familiarity or expertise in those areas.

This approach often resonates with autocratic, transactional, pacesetting, and bureaucratic leadership styles. These styles share a common emphasis on control, structured processes, and clear expectations, which align well with the needs of M1 team members.

Approach 2: Selling, explaining and coaching

This aligns with team members who are at a developing maturity level (M2). These individuals typically have high levels of enthusiasm and commitment, but they lack the competence or experience necessary to effectively execute tasks.

1. **Enhanced two-way communication** Unlike the more directive Approach 1, this involves more interactive communication. As well as giving instructions, the leader explains or "sells" the rationale behind decisions and tasks.
2. **The leader as "coach"** The focus is on developing skills and understanding via a supportive and collaborative approach. Coaching requires giving clear directions and objectives.
3. **Building confidence** When team members understand the "why" behind tasks, they feel more involved and invested in their roles. Boosting confidence fosters a sense of ownership and motivation.

The selling, explaining, and coaching approach is ideal for encouraging team members who are eager to learn. Giving clear explanations and providing hands-on guidance allows leaders to facilitate skills development, while still maintaining the enthusiasm and commitment of the team.

This approach aligns with leadership styles that emphasize employee growth and empowerment. Focusing on both individual and team development ensures that team members are competent and motivated to take on future challenges.

> The selling, explaining, and coaching approach is ideal for encouraging team members who are eager to learn.

Approach 3: Participating, facilitating, and collaborating

This is a strategic approach for team members who have a mature level of development (M3). These individuals typically possess both skill and competence, but they may vary in their levels of confidence and motivation.

1. **Collaborative decision-making** A shared decision-making process requires collaborating with team members in order to arrive at decisions collectively.
2. **The leader as a facilitator** Being a facilitator involves supporting team members, encouraging teamwork, and creating an environment where everyone has a voice and feels empowered to contribute.
3. **Enhancing confidence and motivation** Involving team members in the decision-making process boosts morale. When leaders demonstrate trust in their capabilities, it increases self-confidence and commitment to their tasks.

The participating, facilitating and collaborating approach works best with competent teams who may need encouragement or guidance to fully apply their skills and take on more responsibility. Individuals at the M3 maturity level are often in a transitional phase; they have developed the necessary skills, but they may be hesitant to take the initiative or make decisions independently. This approach provides a supportive framework that allows them to confidently contribute and take on more active roles. When decision-making becomes participative, it builds confidence. As such, it is a key component of democratic leadership.

> The participating, facilitating, and collaborating approach works best with competent teams.

This approach also suits transformational and visionary leadership styles, which focus on empowering team members and motivating them towards a shared vision.

Approach 4: Delegating, empowering, and monitoring

This approach is specifically designed for team members who have reached a high level of maturity (M4). These individuals are characterized by their competence, strong motivation, and the ability to work independently with minimal supervision.

1. **Autonomy and trust** Allowing team members to take ownership of tasks and decision-making processes indicates that you trust their capabilities and judgment.
2. **Minimal supervision** In this hands-off approach, leaders monitor progress and outcomes, but they only intervene when necessary. This empowers team members to take responsibility for their work.
3. **Provide support** Despite delegating responsibilities, leaders remain accessible. They provide support, guidance, and resources when requested, ensuring team members have what they need to succeed.

SITUATIONAL LEADERSHIP: A FOUR-STYLE APPROACH

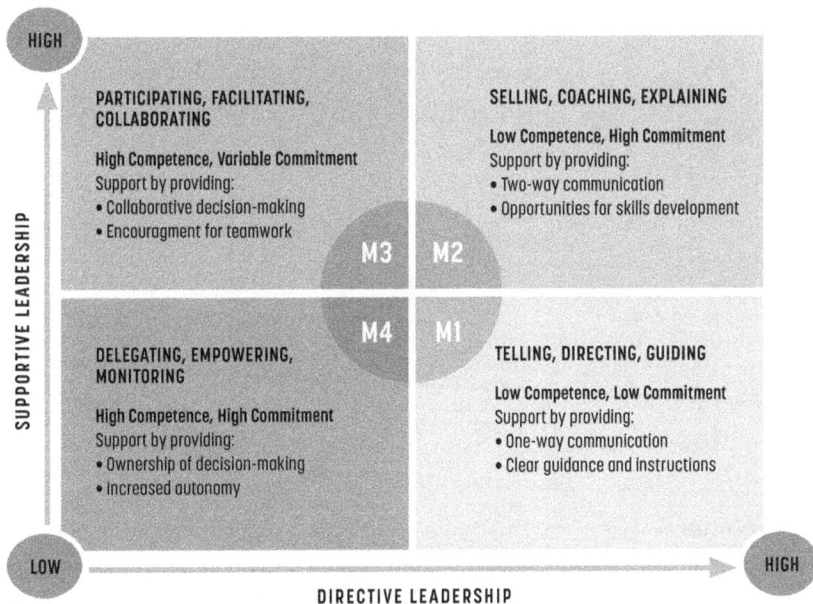

51

Delegating, empowering and monitoring promotes self-reliance and encourages team members to take the initiative. It prepares individuals for future leadership roles and enhances their contribution to the organization. Team members at the M4 maturity level require less hands-on management and more strategic support. This approach offers the correct mix of autonomy and support to help highly motivated and committed individuals excel.

This approach is most closely associated with laissez-faire leadership, with its emphasis on individual autonomy and minimal direct supervision. However, there are also elements of democratic leadership.

Seeing situational leadership through different lenses

Adopting a situational mindset comes with challenges. A situational leader needs a high degree of emotional intelligence (EI) to correctly gauge their team's abilities and morale. They must be able to swiftly analyze a situation and determine the most effective leadership style to apply. Situational leadership also requires openness and flexibility, and a willingness to shift your approach as necessary. Despite this, situational leadership can be highly effective. By adapting to the specifics of the situation, as well as the needs of team members, situational leaders can guide their teams to success in a variety of circumstances.

> A situational leader needs a high degree of emotional intelligence to correctly gauge their team's abilities and morale.

Understanding your unique leadership style impacts your approach to managing and leading others. It shapes the way you communicate, make decisions, and handle crises. It also allows you to play to your strengths, work on areas for self-development, and function more effectively within a team.

Self-aware leaders recognize their biases and are equipped to manage or eliminate them. By recognizing when your style is helpful, or may be hindering your team's progress, you can consciously adjust your approach and become more versatile.

To evaluate your situational leadership approach, rate each statement from 1–4 according to how well it applies to you (1 being least applicable; 4 being most applicable). Do not use the same rating more than once.

A. I provide clear, precise instructions and closely supervise tasks that have been assigned.
B. I encourage open dialogue and explain my decisions to my team.
C. I promote collaboration and often delegate decision-making.
D. I trust my team to work autonomously and give them the freedom to execute tasks their way.

If your scores are highest in:

A: You lean towards the Telling, Directing or Guiding approach. As an autocratic or bureaucratic leader, you are comfortable with transactional and pacesetting leadership.
B: Your style favors coaching leadership, with its Selling, Coaching, or Explaining approach.
C: Your democratic style makes you a visionary and transformational leader. You align most closely with the Participating, Facilitating, or Collaborating approach.
D: Your laissez-faire leadership style resonates with the Delegating, Empowering, or Monitoring approach.

Assessing your leadership style

Leadership is an introspective journey that requires continuous self-examination and deep self-awareness. Before you can use your knowledge to inspire and guide others, you first need to understand yourself, your motivations, and your strengths and weaknesses. To gain deeper insights into your leadership style and its impacts, make use of the most applicable professionally developed assessment models discussed below. These differing perspectives can offer profound insights into your leadership style, and provide a framework for your growth as a leader.

As you explore, remember that self-awareness is an ongoing process. Continual reflection and self-assessment will allow you to deepen your understanding of yourself as a leader and, ultimately, guide your personal development and growth.

Psychological assessment

Psychological assessment gives insight into our inherent character (personality) traits. Gaining a holistic understanding of your leadership style allows you to leverage your strengths, or address areas for growth. Knowing your leadership style can help shape your interactions with others, and inform your decision-making or conflict resolution processes. You will learn more about these valuable tools in Golden Star 3, which focuses on enhancing leaders' capacity to navigate challenges.

- **DISC Assessment** This categorizes behaviors into Dominance, Influence, Steadiness, and Conscientiousness. It helps leaders identify traits such as decisiveness, persuasiveness, reliability, or detail-orientation, and uses them to tailor their leadership approach.
- **Myers-Briggs Type Indicator (MBTI)** This reveals how we perceive things by assessing preferences in the way we derive our emotional energy (Extraversion/Introversion), process information (Sensing/Intuition), make decisions (Thinking/Feeling), and deal with the world around us (Judging/Perceiving). Myers-Briggs gives insight into how behavioral preferences have an impact on leadership style.
- **Predictive Index Behavioral Assessment** This helps leaders understand what drives their normal workplace behaviors, including their approach to decision-making, and how they interact with their team members.

Emotional assessment

Emotional assessment is pivotal for leaders who want to enhance their emotional intelligence (EI), a key aspect of effective leadership. Viewing yourself through an emotional lens forces you to consider your ability to recognize, understand, and manage your own emotions, and empathically interact with others.

Leaders need to gauge how they will respond under pressure. How will you cope with your teams' emotional needs, or manage your reactions in a stressful situation? Emotional assessment provides valuable insights, helping leaders refine their level of emotional awareness and empathy. Understanding and enhancing their EI lets leaders create a work environment characterized by empathy, effective communication, and strong interpersonal relationships, all of which are vital for organizational success. You will find more on emotional intelligence in Golden Star 6.

- **Emotional Intelligence Appraisal (Me Edition)** By measuring emotional intelligence on four core skills: self-awareness, self-management, social awareness, and relationship management, this model helps leaders understand their capacity to manage their emotions and navigate social complexities within their teams.
- **Mayer-Salovey-Caruso Emotional Intelligence Test (MSCEIT)** This evaluates emotional intelligence through emotion-based problem-solving. It provides insights into how effectively leaders use emotions to facilitate thinking and understand complex emotional information, which aids in decision-making and leadership strategy development.
- **Bar-On Emotional Quotient Inventory (EQ-i)** This model takes a deep dive into the leader's ability to perceive, express, understand, and regulate emotions.

Behavioral assessment

Behavioral assessment provides insights into how our behavior can influence team morale and overall effectiveness. It is essential for leaders seeking to understand how they react in various situations. Assessing your behavior begins with answering questions about your leadership style. Are you naturally inclined to take charge, or do you excel in a supportive role? Do you thrive in collaborative settings, or prefer to work independently? Understanding these responses helps you recognize behavior patterns that might negatively affect decision-making, productivity, and collaboration within your team.

- **The Hogan Personality Inventory (HPI)** The HPI provides insights into how a leader's personality traits, such as ambition, sociability, and sensitivity, manifest in their everyday work scenarios. Understanding these traits allows leaders to enhance their interpersonal skills and adapt their behavior for maximum effectiveness.
- **16 Personality Factor Questionnaire (16PF)** This evaluates a range of normal adult personality traits, such as decision-making styles, problem-solving abilities, and interpersonal interactions, across 16 different scales. The insights enable leaders to tailor their approach based on their unique personality profile.
- **Minnesota Multiphasic Personality Inventory (MMPI)** This model helps leaders understand complex aspects of their personality, such as assertiveness, stress tolerance, and adaptability to change, which are crucial in leadership roles.

Social assessment

Social assessment seeks to understand and refine our interactions within social and professional networks. By considering our communication style, approach to conflict resolution, and ability to connect with others, it evaluates how leaders engage with their team members. Answers to questions such as: "Are you a consensus builder or more authoritative?" or "Do you cultivate a broad, diverse network or do you operate within a close-knit group?" will inform your approach to social interactions and can be applied to how you guide and interact with your team.

- **Social Styles Model** This assesses social behavior in business contexts, categorizing individuals into one of four social styles: Analytical, Driving, Amiable, or Expressive. It helps leaders understand their preferred style of interaction and how they adapt to various social situations, enhancing team communication and collaboration.
- **FIRO-B (Fundamental Interpersonal Relations Orientation-Behavior)** This assessment focuses on a leader's typical behaviors towards others, as well as their social needs in areas, such as inclusion, control, and affection. Insights into how you form relationships, your

approach to teamwork, and your need for interaction, can be utilized to develop effective interpersonal strategies.

- **Thomas-Kilmann Conflict Mode Instrument (TKI)** This assesses different conflict-handling styles to understand their impact on interpersonal and group dynamics. It equips leaders with the skills to navigate conflict effectively, fostering a harmonious work environment.

Ethical assessment

Ethical assessment is fundamental for leaders who want to align their actions with their core values and principles. It encourages leaders to consider their ethical reasoning and decision-making, and how their moral compass guides their leadership style. Understanding one's ethical stance helps ensure that decisions and actions not only achieve results, but that they are also grounded in fairness, integrity, and social responsibility.

> Ethical assessment is fundamental for leaders who want to align their actions with their core values and principles.

Good leaders must ponder their approach to ethical dilemmas. Do you incline towards a strong sense of justice and equality, or are your decisions driven by results and outcomes? The process of aligning leadership actions with personal and organizational values will ensure that your decisions not only drive success, but that they also uphold the highest ethical standards.

- **Defining Issues Test (DIT)** This test assesses ethical and moral reasoning. It provides insights into how leaders navigate complex ethical dilemmas and the impact of these decisions on their leadership.
- **Ethical Lens Inventory** By taking careful inventory, leaders will recognize their ethical blind spots and strengths. Gaining an understanding of personal ethics and values allows leaders to make more balanced and principled decisions.
- **Moral Foundations Questionnaire (MFQ)** By evaluating base ethical values and moral reasoning, the MFQ provides an understanding of the underlying moral foundations that influence a leader's decisions, enabling them to lead with a more nuanced and ethical perspective.

Refining your leadership style

Leadership is a dynamic and complex process that begins with self-awareness. Your leadership style allows you to lead with intention, clarity, and understanding, ensuring your team feels guided, valued, and motivated to do their best. By understanding your style, you can more easily navigate your role, build stronger relationships with your team members, make better-informed decisions, and steer your organization towards its goals with greater clarity and confidence.

Identifying your leadership style is just the first step. The next step is to develop and refine it. Here are some suggestions:

1. **Leverage your strengths** Once you have identified your leadership style, play to your strengths. If you're good at delegating and empowering, find opportunities to put those skills to use. If your strength is in coaching and explaining, focus on situations where you can mentor others. Be mindful not to overplay your strengths.

2. **Work on your areas for development** Every leadership style has its shortcomings. Once you know yours, find ways to address them. If you have a tendency to direct and tell, try to cultivate better listening skills, and be more open to input from others.

3. **Seek feedback** Regular feedback from your peers and team members can provide valuable insights into how your leadership style is perceived, and its effectiveness.

4. **Learn from others** Observe leaders who have different styles from your own. You can learn a lot from how they handle various situations, and which leadership practices they adopt.

5. **Pursue professional development** Attend workshops, seminars, or coaching sessions to discover new tools and techniques that will enhance your leadership style.

6. **Practice flexibility** Remember the principles of different leadership styles and situational leadership: The best leaders are those who adapt their style to suit the situation. While it is good to know your dominant style, don't become rigid.

STORY IN PRACTICE

Finding your leadership style

Noah Sanders was the charismatic and ambitious founder of a tech startup. Although he was an expert in his field, Noah was a relatively inexperienced leader, and while his visionary brilliance had won the respect of investors and customers alike, his team did not seem similarly "wowed". Despite his best attempts to guide them, they would question his directives, and frequently suggest other paths or solutions. Noah couldn't understand why they were unwilling to follow his lead.

After a particularly uncomfortable meeting, Noah approached Ed, who'd been with him from the start. "What's going on?" Noah asked. "If you really want to know, it's your leadership style," Ed said. "You constantly give orders, but you never want to listen to what anyone else thinks. You've recruited some top industry talent, but you treat them as if you were the only smart one in the room."

"It's your leadership style." These frank words gave Noah the wake-up call he needed. After some reflection, he realized that if he wanted his company to succeed, he had to acquire a new set of skills. The first step was to learn about different leadership styles, and discover which was right for him. This was a game-changer for Noah. Once he understood that his tendency to dictate terms and make unilateral decisions marked him as an autocratic leader, he recognized the need to adapt his leadership style to the levels of competence in his team. As Ed pointed out, Noah had handpicked some of the best people in the industry to join his startup. It was time to show them the respect they deserved.

Noah sought feedback from his team leaders, as well as his mentors in the tech world, using their comments to assess his strengths and weaknesses, and evaluate his attitudes and values. He set his sights on becoming a transformational leader; someone who could inspire others through a shared vision. He wanted his company to be seen as an enterprise that stood for personal growth and a spirit of innovation.

He reassigned the responsibilities of his top team, matching their roles to their individual knowledge, skills, and experience. He gave the leaders more autonomy and paved the way for them to set goals for their teams.

Noah's personal challenge was to develop his own leadership style. Discovering the Four Approaches to Situational Leadership helped him understand that while he had been mostly "telling and directing", he needed to focus on "participating and facilitating", and "delegating and empowering". To accomplish this, he took deliberate actions. He set clear expectations, promoted open communication, and encouraged and accepted feedback. Most importantly, he empowered his team members to make decisions. He remained mindful of his interactions with others, and kept fine-tuning his approach based on the feedback he received.

It wasn't long before the new strategy paid off. As people took ownership of their tasks, productivity soared, and a new creative energy resulted in exciting technological innovations. Performance improved across all divisions, team leaders were more engaged, and there was noticeably less frustration at all levels. Witnessing the change in his company, Noah finally felt that he was becoming the leader he should have been all along.

By embracing situational leadership, Noah Sanders went from being a tech genius with autocratic tendencies, to a leader who made an effort to understand his team's needs, and adapt his style to the specific situation or circumstances. His story demonstrates how anyone, irrespective of expertise or experience, can become an effective leader.

SELF-REFLECTION PIT STOP

Scan the QR code or visit drtomdreyer.com/tools to download your e-toolkit.

Leadership styles

Part 1: Understanding leadership styles

1. Reflect on the different leadership styles discussed in this Golden Star. Which style do you identify with most closely? Provide specific examples of how you have demonstrated the characteristics of this style in your leadership.
2. Do you find certain leadership styles challenging or difficult to relate to? Why do you think this is? Could understanding these styles better improve your leadership capabilities?

Part 2: Unpacking situational leadership

1. Consider the four approaches to situational leadership (Telling/ Directing, Selling/Coaching, Participating/Facilitating, Delegating/ Empowering). Have you used each one in your leadership practice? If you have not used a particular approach, why not, and in what future situations might it be useful?

2. How comfortable are you with adapting your leadership approach to different situations? Can you think of a situation where you effectively adjusted your approach? What about a situation where you could have been more adaptable?

Part 3: Determining your leadership style

1. If you took a professionally developed assessment, or conducted a self-rating exercise, were you surprised by the results? Why, or why not?

2. Reflect on feedback you have received from your team or colleagues. Does it align with your self-assessment of your leadership style?

Part 4: Developing your leadership style

1. Based on your reflections above, identify one or two strengths that apply to your predominant leadership style. How can you further leverage these strengths?

2. Identify one or two areas where you could enhance your leadership style. What specific actions can you take to work on these areas?

Part 5: Set SMART goals

Based on your reflections, set two or three SMART goals to refine your leadership style. For example, if as a coaching leader, you have identified a need to be more proactive, your SMART goal might be: "Within the next six weeks, I will identify three areas (or issues) where my team, or individual team members, need additional coaching, and I will set set up coaching sessions for them."

This Golden Star has taken you on a journey through various leadership styles and approaches, highlighting their strengths and shortcomings. We delved into the concept of situational leadership, emphasizing the importance of flexibility and adaptability. By regularly revisiting your reflections and goals, you'll be able to track your progress and make any necessary adjustments. But remember, leadership is about creating symphonies, not solo performances.

Endnotes

1   Study on Neuroplasticity and Leadership Learning: Boyatzis, R. E., Rochford, K., & Jack, A. I. (2014). Antagonistic neural networks underlying differentiated leadership roles. *Frontiers in Human Neuroscience*, 8, 114.
    Study on Adaptability and Leadership Development: Di Stefano, G., Gino, F., Pisano, G., & Staats, B. R. (2016). Learning by thinking: Overcoming the bias for action through reflection. *Harvard Business School NOM Unit Working Paper No. 14-093.*

GOLDEN STAR

3

UNDERSTANDING YOUR TEAM

Golden Star 3 explores different ways of understanding your team. Making use of personality assessments, as well as tailoring your approach for different generational groups, helps leaders accommodate the uniqueness of individual team members. Once you understand what drives people, you can adapt your leadership style to maximize their potential, thereby building a stronger and better-functioning team.

Personality assessments

The hallmark of exceptional leaders is their ability to discern their team members' distinct strengths and weaknesses. The ability to recognize individual personalities and preferred behavioral styles is a pivotal skill with tangible repercussions for team morale, productivity, and overall success. Discernment equips leaders with the capacity to allocate tasks that correspond to individuals' innate capabilities and inclinations. This approach not only optimizes productivity, it also raises levels of employee satisfaction and engagement.

Personality assessments offer invaluable insights into how your team members process information, make decisions, and engage with others. By decoding the outcomes, leaders can tailor their strategies to effectively engage, inspire, and motivate each team member. Remember that, as individuals, we are all different. As a leader, it is important to respect these differences.

> The hallmark of exceptional leaders is their ability to discern their team members' distinct strengths and weaknesses.

Each person has a unique brain, a unique personality, and a unique set of strengths. Our individual brain structures and neurochemical processes contribute significantly to shaping our behaviors, preferences, and ultimately, our personalities. Personality traits, such as introversion or extroversion, have been linked to differing patterns of neural activation and neurotransmitter levels. Understanding personality traits can help you create a more effective and harmonious team.

The Myers-Briggs Type Indicator

The Myers-Briggs Type Indicator (MBTI) is a psychological assessment that was developed during World War II by Isabel Briggs Myers and her mother, Katharine Cook Briggs. Based on Carl Jung's theory of psychological types, 'Myers-Briggs' is widely used in leadership and team building, due to its effectiveness in understanding and managing human behaviors. The MBTI is based on four dimensions (or "dichotomies").

1. **Extroverts (E) vs. Introverts (I)** This dimension represents how individuals direct their energy. Extroverts are naturally energized by interacting with others and the external world. They think out loud and are often action-oriented. Introverts are energized by spending time alone, or socializing in small groups. They prefer to think things through before speaking or acting.

2. **Sensors (S) vs. Intuitives (N)** This dimension relates to how individuals prefer to take in information. Sensors are pragmatic and down-to-earth, focusing on the details and realities of the situation. They prefer concrete, practical information. Intuitives focus on the big picture and future possibilities. They are drawn to abstract concepts and enjoy innovative ideas and challenging the status quo.

3. **Thinkers (T) vs. Feelers (F)** This dimension deals with how individuals make decisions. Thinkers make decisions based on logic and objective analysis. They are focused on fairness and are generally task-oriented. Feelers make decisions based on personal values and how their decisions will impact others. They are more people-oriented and are focused on harmony and cooperation.

4. **Judgers (J) vs. Perceivers (P)** This dimension represents how individuals prefer to live their lives. Judgers like structure and organization. They are typically decisive, planned and enjoy a sense of closure. Perceivers prefer to keep their options open. They are flexible, adaptable, and comfortable with change.

THE MYERS-BRIGGS TYPE INDICATOR (MBTI)

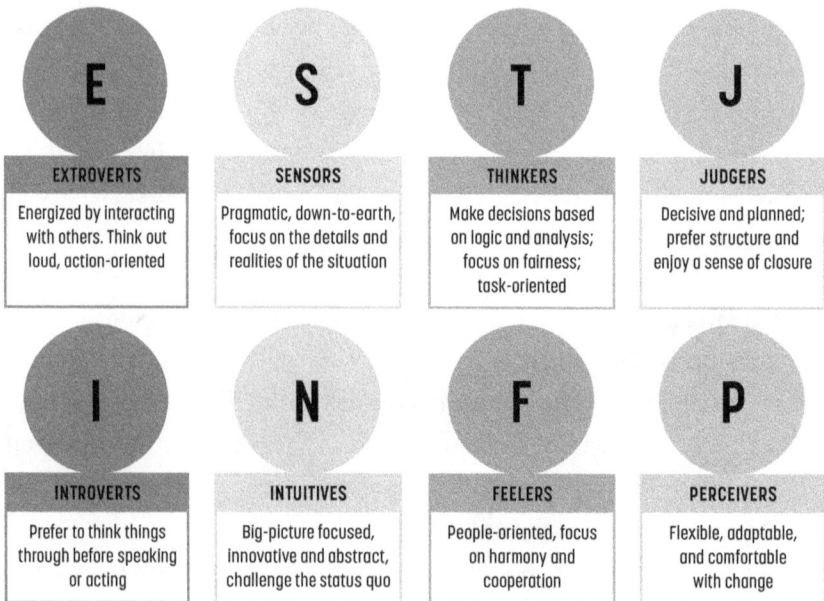

E	S	T	J
EXTROVERTS	**SENSORS**	**THINKERS**	**JUDGERS**
Energized by interacting with others. Think out loud, action-oriented	Pragmatic, down-to-earth, focus on the details and realities of the situation	Make decisions based on logic and analysis; focus on fairness; task-oriented	Decisive and planned; prefer structure and enjoy a sense of closure

I	N	F	P
INTROVERTS	**INTUITIVES**	**FEELERS**	**PERCEIVERS**
Prefer to think things through before speaking or acting	Big-picture focused, innovative and abstract, challenge the status quo	People-oriented, focus on harmony and cooperation	Flexible, adaptable, and comfortable with change

Based on the combination of these four dimensions, we have 16 personality types, each represented by four letters. For example, ISTJ individuals are Introverts, Sensors, Thinkers, and Judgers. This would mean they are quiet, serious, practical, orderly, and logical. As a leader, you can apply strategies that utilize Myers-Briggs personality types to various aspects of team leadership, including:

- **Appreciating individual differences** Understanding the MBTI will help leaders to appreciate the diversity of their team members. It is important to accept that there's no "best" personality type; each has its strengths and challenges.
- **Improving communication** Recognizing each team member's unique personality type allows leaders to adjust their communication style to better match different personalities and preferences. For example, an Extrovert leader could take steps to provide opportunities for Introvert team members to express their thoughts.

- **Enhancing team dynamics** Acknowledging different personality types can help leaders build balanced, effective teams. For example, a team with a mix of Sensors and Intuitives will be well-equipped to handle both the details and the big picture.
- **Fostering personal development** By knowing their own MBTI type, leaders can gain insights into their leadership style, including their strengths and potential blind spots. This can guide their personal development journey.

While the MBTI provides valuable insights, it's important to remember that it is a tool for understanding, not a box in which to confine people. Furthermore, it does not measure competence or capability; it merely highlights different preferences. Individuals are complex and unique, and their personality might not fit neatly into one type. As a leader, your role is to blend diverse styles into a harmonious and productive team.

The DISC model

This personality assessment tool is widely used in leadership and organizational settings. Developed by American psychologist William Marston in 1928, it focuses on predicting behaviors and interactions in different environments. The acronym DISC represents four personality types:

1. **Dominant (D)** types prefer direct, decisive action. They are assertive, competitive, results-oriented, and enjoy challenges. If not managed effectively, they may come across as impatient, blunt, or even aggressive.
2. **Influential (I)** types love interacting with others. They are impulsive, enthusiastic, persuasive, and animated. Usually great team players, they can inspire and motivate. However, they can also be perceived as impulsive, disorganized, and lacking focus, especially by the more results-oriented "D" types.
3. **Steady (S)** types are stable and supportive. Reliable, and consistent, they express patience, persistence, and are often excellent listeners. They can resist change and be seen as too passive or overly accommodating.

4. **Compliant (C)** types are careful and conscientious. Analytical, and detail-oriented, they value accuracy. They are likely to be diplomatic, systematic, and good at ensuring quality. Their high standards can make them overly critical, or indecisive.

THE DISC MODEL

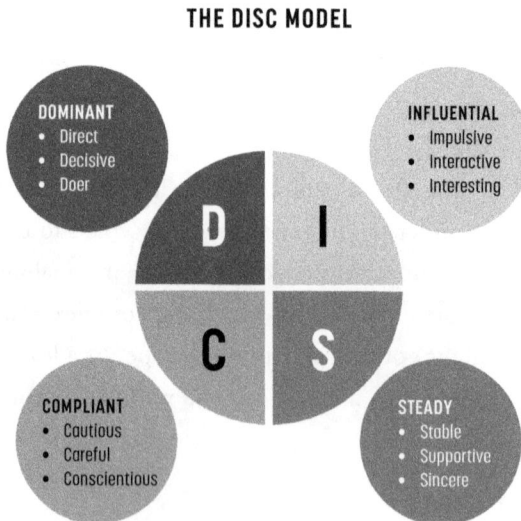

Leaders can use the DISC model to improve their effectiveness by building strategies around individual DISC personality types.

- **Tailor communication strategies** Knowing your team members' DISC types can lead to more effective communication. For example, "D" types prefer concise, to-the-point communication, while "I" types appreciate conversations that are both engaging and collaborative.
- **Assign roles effectively** By recognizing the strengths of each DISC style, leaders can assign tasks that align with team members' natural inclinations. For example, "C" types are great for roles requiring precision and accuracy, while "I" types shine in roles that require collaboration and interpersonal communication.
- **Improve conflict resolution** Use your knowledge of DISC styles to mediate conflicts and foster understanding among team members. For example, "D" types might clash with "S" types because of their different pace, and their attitudes to risk.

- **Facilitate personal and team growth** Understanding their own DISC style and its implications allows leaders to work on their own areas of improvement. Initiating a team discussion about DISC styles can lead to increased self-awareness and mutual understanding, thus strengthening team cohesion.

Remember, no DISC style is better or worse than the others; they are just different. Each style has its strengths and its areas for improvement. For a leader, the DISC model is a powerful tool for fostering a harmonious, productive and understanding work environment. Bear in mind that people are more complex than any model can conceive, so use DISC as a guide rather than a definitive measure of personality.

The Enneagram

The Enneagram approach looks at individual behaviors, as well as our fundamental fears and desires. This profound tool, which allows leaders to understand themselves and their team members more intimately, enhances synergy and interpersonal dynamics within teams.

The Enneagram presents nine unique types, representing worldviews and archetypes that resonate with an individual's thought patterns, feelings, and actions in relation to the world, others, and themselves.

1. **Perfectionists** Ethical, dependable, productive, and strive for improvement and perfection. They yearn to live right, better themselves and others, and avoid error and culpability. Neuroscience suggests that, with their constant striving for correctness, Perfectionists might show increased activity in the brain's prefrontal regions, which are responsible for planning and decision-making.
2. **Helpers** Exude care, generosity, and a propensity to please others. Their quest for love drives them, and they thrive on being needed. It is likely that Helpers have a highly active oxytocin system, the hormone often associated with bonding and social relationships.
3. **Achievers** Adaptable, driven, conscious of their image, and in relentless pursuit of success and admiration. They may exhibit increased

71

dopamine activity, which plays a significant role in the brain's reward and motivation circuits.

4. **Individualists** Introspective, romantic, and expressive. They seek to understand their unique identity and aspire towards authenticity. This could be associated with heightened activity in the regions of the brain related to self-reflection and emotional processing.

5. **Investigators** Perceptive and innovative, yet secretive and isolated. They crave knowledge, but fear a sense of helplessness or incapacity. They might have active brain networks that are related to their facility for problem-solving and information processing.

6. **Loyalists** Committed and reliable, yet anxious and suspicious. They seek security and fear being unsupported or unguided. This may tie into the brain's amygdala activity, which is responsible for processing fear and anxiety.

7. **Enthusiasts** Extroverted, spontaneous, and versatile. They desire satisfaction and contentment, and dislike discomfort. They may show heightened activity in the brain's reward pathways.

8. **Challengers** Self-confident, decisive, and confrontational. They aim to safeguard themselves and exercise control over their surroundings. This might link to higher testosterone levels, often associated with dominance and competitiveness.

9. **Peacemakers** Receptive and reassuring, although they can be complacent and resigned. They crave peace and tend to avoid conflict. This could be related to heightened activity in the part of the brain linked to introspection and a "wandering mind".

Leaders can use the Enneagram to gain insight into their team members' motivations. In common with other personality assessment models, the Enneagram is a tool designed to foster deeper self-understanding and empathy for others. It should not be used to stereotype or limit individuals. Every Enneagram type has unique strengths and challenges; embracing this diversity can help leaders to assemble more effective, harmonious teams.

Leaders can use the Enneagram to gain insight into their team members' motivations.

THE ENNEAGRAM APPROACH

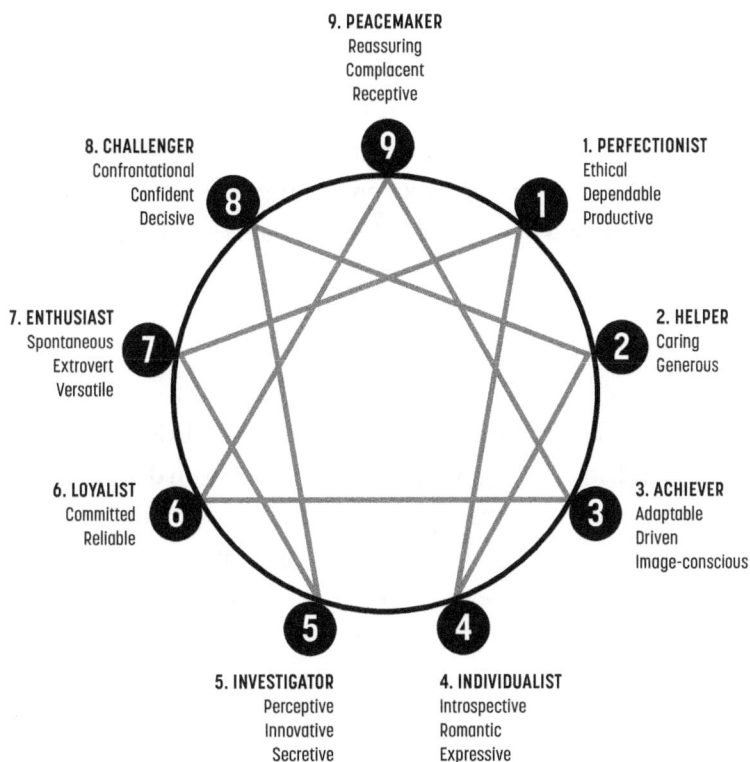

9. PEACEMAKER
Reassuring
Complacent
Receptive

8. CHALLENGER
Confrontational
Confident
Decisive

1. PERFECTIONIST
Ethical
Dependable
Productive

7. ENTHUSIAST
Spontaneous
Extrovert
Versatile

2. HELPER
Caring
Generous

6. LOYALIST
Committed
Reliable

3. ACHIEVER
Adaptable
Driven
Image-conscious

5. INVESTIGATOR
Perceptive
Innovative
Secretive

4. INDIVIDUALIST
Introspective
Romantic
Expressive

- **Individualize your leadership approach** Not everyone responds favorably to the same leadership style. For example, Achievers (Type 3) are motivated by success, so setting clear objectives and acknowledging their accomplishments will likely yield positive outcomes.
- **Improve communication** Helpers (Type 2) value relationships and assisting others, so appreciating their efforts in supporting the team can strike a resonant chord.
- **Professional development** Investigators (Type 5) are often oriented towards knowledge, and will probably thrive on opportunities to learn and apply new skills.

The CLPS model

The Comprehensive Leadership Personality Spectrum (CLPS) enhances a leader's knowledge of personal dynamics. This assessment tool, which I developed, amalgamates key elements of the MBTI, DISC, and Enneagram personality models. Backed by neuroscience, CLPS is underpinned by a four-dimensional matrix: Mindset, Behavior, Core Desires and Fears, and Motivation, with each dimension contributing to our understanding of personality traits, and how to utilize these in our leadership practice.

Mindset: Introvert vs. Extrovert

Inspired by MBTI, this dimension focuses on how individuals obtain their energy and recharge. In neuroscience, this is linked with dopamine, part of the brain's reward system that influences our response to stimuli.[1]

Introverts tend to be contemplative and reserved. Their reactive dopamine system means they often prefer solitary activities over social ones. Extroverts, who are less sensitive to dopamine, are outgoing, thrive in social settings, and actively seek stimulating environments. Understanding this enables leaders to create work environments that respect individual needs for solitude or interaction, and makes the most of each team member's innate personality traits.

Behavior: Task-oriented vs. People-oriented

Based on the DISC model, this dimension examines whether individuals are more focused on accomplishing tasks or building relationships. These neuroscientific distinctions highlight the diverse approaches to problem-solving and interpersonal dynamics that can occur in teams.[2]

Task-oriented individuals are associated with left-brain hemisphere dominance, which is linked to logical thinking, organization, and analytical skills. They excel in environments that demand structure and logic. People-oriented individuals, on the other hand, prioritize relationships and personal interactions. They exhibit dominance in the right-brain hemisphere, known for emotional processing, intuition, and creativity.

The CLPS framework allows leaders to acknowledge different working preferences among their team members and enables them to tailor their approach to align with these tendencies, resulting in better communication and improved efficiency.

Core desires and fears: Identity, connection, and security

Influenced by the Enneagram model, this dimension delves into emotions, and how they drive us. Core desires and fears, such as identity, connection, and security, are intricately linked to our brain's limbic system, which is the epicenter of emotion.[3]

Our concept of identity is linked to the prefrontal cortex, an area of the brain that plays a role in self-awareness and personality expression, helping individuals understand and define their identity within a social context. The desire for connection is influenced by oxytocin, the social bonding hormone that enhances our ability to form and maintain social bonds. Our need for security is governed by the amygdala, which processes emotions such as fear and anxiety. Our requirement for stability and safety is influenced by the way we perceive or react to threats.

Recognizing these neural underpinnings helps leaders understand what drives individuals. By applying the CLPS framework, leaders can accommodate basic desires or fears, and create a supportive work environment that enhances effectiveness.

Motivation: Achievement, affiliation, and power

This dimension looks at what motivates individuals. This could be the pursuit of excellence, a desire to meet goals, or a need to form connections. Neuroscientific studies reveal how motivation plays a role in shaping our aspirations and behaviors.[4]

The drive for achievement (such as meeting goals, or excelling in what we do) is linked to dopamine, the brain's reward chemical. Because this neurotransmitter is activated when a goal is reached or a task is completed, it reinforces behaviors associated with success and accomplishment. Achievement thus becomes a cycle of action, reward, and renewed motivation to pursue further goals.

The need for affiliation (making connections) is rooted in the brain's social circuitry, particularly the prefrontal cortex, which governs social decision-making and empathy. Affiliation enhances our capacity to build relationships and foster social connections.

The quest for power involves the interplay between testosterone and cortisol, hormones that respond to success or failure. Hormonal changes can influence behaviors related to dominance, competition, and social hierarchy. Understanding how these manifest can give leaders insight into what motivates their team members, allowing them to cultivate a work environment that aligns with their intrinsic motivations. This might include providing the right incentives, or offering appropriate feedback.

COMPREHENSIVE LEADERSHIP PERSONALITY SPECTRUM (CLPS)

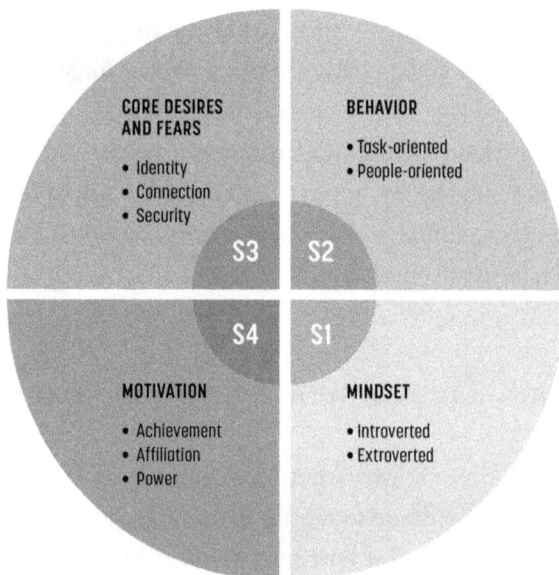

CORE DESIRES AND FEARS
- Identity
- Connection
- Security

BEHAVIOR
- Task-oriented
- People-oriented

S3 S2

S4 S1

MOTIVATION
- Achievement
- Affiliation
- Power

MINDSET
- Introverted
- Extroverted

Applying the CLPS model

Having an understanding of personal dynamics allows you to communicate more effectively with your team members, tap into their strengths, guide them in a manner that resonates with their personalities, and motivate them to perform at their best. Leaders who choose the CLPS model need to follow a series of practical steps:

1. **Conduct personality assessments** Use the questionnaire to evaluate yourself and your team members. Repeat the exercise periodically to capture any changes in personality traits.
2. **Analyze the results** Compare the scores within each dimension to understand dominant traits. A high score in one aspect versus its counterpart (such as Introvert vs. Extrovert) indicates a stronger inclination towards that trait.
3. **Tailor your approach** Based on the results, leaders can adapt their communication, delegation, and motivational strategies. For example, a task-oriented individual might thrive with clear, structured objectives, while a people-oriented person may excel in roles that require collaboration and team interaction.
4. **Provide a supportive environment** Create a work culture that respects individual differences. For instance, provide quiet workspaces for introverts, or encourage extroverts to engage in team-building activities.
5. **Generate individual development plans** Use insights from the CLPS model to guide personal development conversations. Offer opportunities and challenges that align with individual motivations and strengths.
6. **Observation** Beyond the questionnaire, leaders should observe day-to-day interactions and adjust their approach as needed. Ongoing assessment ensures that leadership remains dynamic, and responsive to team changes.

The CLPS model is a powerful tool for leaders who seek to harness diverse personalities and create a harmonious and motivated team which, in turn, leads to improved productivity and job satisfaction.

CLPS Personality Assessment

How to use the questionnaire:
1. Rate every statement on a scale from 1–5 (where 1 = Strongly Disagree, 2 = Disagree, 3 = Neutral, 4 = Agree, 5 = Strongly Agree). Answer as honestly as possible to get an accurate assessment.
2. After rating all statements in a section, add up the scores for each personality type (for example, Introvert / Extrovert, Task-oriented / People-oriented). Enter your totals in the space provided.
3. Complete all the sections to gain a comprehensive understanding of the personality spectrum.

Digital tool available at drtomdreyer.com/tools

CLPS Personality Assessment		
Mindset: Introvert vs Extrovert		
Trait	**Statement**	**Rating (1-5)**
Introvert	I often prefer spending time alone to recharge.	
	I usually think through my ideas before sharing them.	
	Large social gatherings tend to drain my energy.	
	I prefer working on tasks independently rather than in a group.	
	I find too much social interaction overwhelming.	
	Total for Introvert	

CLPS Personality Assessment		
Mindset: Introvert vs Extrovert		
Trait	Statement	Rating (1-5)
Extrovert	I enjoy engaging in group activities and discussions.	
	I am energized by spending time with others.	
	I often think out loud and express my ideas spontaneously.	
	I thrive in dynamic and social work environments.	
	I prefer collaborative tasks over working alone.	
	Total for Extrovert	
Behavior: Task-oriented vs People-oriented		
Trait	Statement	Rating (1-5)
Task-oriented	I focus on achieving specific goals and objectives.	
	I am comfortable working in structured and organized settings.	
	I value efficiency and productivity in my work.	
	I prefer making decisions based on data and logic.	
	I am detail-oriented and meticulous in my tasks.	
	Total for Task-oriented	
People-oriented	I prioritize building and maintaining relationships at work.	
	I value teamwork and collaboration.	
	I am attentive to the emotions and needs of others.	
	I enjoy roles that require communication and interpersonal skills.	
	I often make decisions based on their impact on the people involved.	
	Total for People-oriented	

Core desires and fears: Identity, connection, and security		
Trait	Statement	Rating (1-5)
Identity	I have a strong sense of who I am and my unique strengths.	
	My personal values and beliefs are important in my life decisions.	
	I seek roles that allow me to express my individuality.	
	Achieving personal goals is a top priority for me.	
	I am motivated by opportunities to develop my personal identity.	
	Total for Identity	

Core desires and fears: Identity, connection, and security		
Trait	Statement	Rating (1-5)
Connection	Building strong relationships is essential to my happiness.	
	I value being part of a community or group.	
	I feel fulfilled when I am able to help or support others.	
	I prioritize the wellbeing and success of my team.	
	I am motivated by opportunities to foster collaboration and teamwork.	
	Total for Connection	
Security	Stability and predictability are important in my work and life.	
	I prefer environments where risks and uncertainties are minimized.	
	Having a clear and structured plan gives me a sense of comfort.	
	I value job security and long-term career planning.	
	I am motivated by roles that provide a sense of safety and security.	
	Total for Security	

Motivation: Achievement, affiliation, and power		
Trait	Statement	Rating (1-5)
Achievement	Accomplishing my goals is a major driver for me.	
	I am motivated by setting and reaching targets.	
	I feel successful when I complete tasks and projects.	
	Recognition for my achievements is important to me.	
	I am constantly looking for ways to improve and excel.	
	Total for Achievement	

Motivation: Achievement, affiliation, and power		
Trait	Statement	Rating (1-5)
Affiliation	Forming close relationships at work is important to me.	
	I enjoy working in teams and collaborating with others.	
	I am motivated by being a part of a group or community.	
	I prioritize harmony and positive relationships in my team.	
	I find satisfaction in being connected and well-liked.	
	Total for Affiliation	
Power	I aspire to be in a position of influence and leadership.	
	Having control over decisions and direction is important to me.	
	I am motivated by opportunities that increase my authority.	
	I enjoy being able to direct and influence the outcome of projects.	
	I feel successful when I can lead and guide others.	
	Total for Power	

Interpreting the results

1. **Identify dominant traits** Within each section, compare the total scores of the trait pairs (for example, Introvert vs. Extrovert). The higher score indicates a stronger inclination towards that particular

trait. If the scores are similar for both traits, it suggests a balanced, versatile personality, with a moderate preference for both traits.

2. **Personality analysis** Combine your insights from all sections to get an overview. This can reveal complex, multifaceted personality profiles.

3. **Application**
   - *Adapt your leadership style* Use the insights to align your leadership approach with the individual traits of team members.
     For example, provide more autonomy to those who score higher in the Achievement trait, or offer collaborative projects for those with high Affiliation scores.
   - *Improve team dynamics* Understanding the diverse personality traits within a team can help you to assign roles, improve communications, and resolve conflicts more effectively.
   - *Personal development* Encourage team members to reflect on their results for self-awareness and professional growth, and use the questionnaire as a tool for personal development planning.

4. **Ongoing assessment** Re-administer the questionnaire periodically. This will allow you to capture evolving personality dynamics or, after significant team changes, to adjust your leadership strategies.

STORY IN PRACTICE

The importance of personality

Marianne Patterson ran a successful micro-lending company. Her staff included ambitious Millennials, tenacious Gen Xers, and experienced Baby Boomers, all of whom had different ways of working. Marianne knew that, in order to merge them into a cohesive team, she needed to acknowledge their individual personalities.

From the many assessment models available, Marianne chose the Comprehensive Leadership Personality Spectrum, with its four dimensions: Mindset, Behavior, Core Desires and Fears, and Motivation. Her first move was to conduct one-on-one meetings with her team. During these open conversations, she used the CLPS personality assessment to ask insightful questions about their working preferences, personal motivations, and professional fears.

As Marianne built up a picture of each individual, she discovered introverts who were task-oriented but had a deep desire for connection, and extroverts who were people-oriented but motivated by a need for achievement. She found that while some team members craved connection and stability, others were motivated by achievements and the potential for meeting goals.

Armed with this knowledge, she tailored her leadership approach to suit each personality type. She provided a supportive environment for introverts, while giving extroverts opportunities to participate in open discussions and brainstorming sessions. Personal development plans allowed high-achievers to set their own goals, while improved collaboration and communication benefited everyone. Ongoing assessment allowed Marianne to remain responsive to changes in team dynamics and adjust the model as necessary.

Marianne's handling of one of the company's most important projects reveals the importance of understanding personality types. Despite a great deal of effort, the project was not going well, and the customer was ready to take his business elsewhere. The team was demoralized by the lack of progress, but seemed unable to find a workable solution. Marianne decided to reconfigure the team by splitting it into two, with one group focusing on implementation, and the other on customer service. She applied her personality assessments to allocate individuals to each team. Task-oriented introverts were assigned to the implementation team, and people-oriented extroverts to the customer service team.

Within weeks, the project was back on track. By harnessing their strengths, both teams delivered the required results. The response was immediate. Employee morale soared, and the customer was delighted. Instead of withdrawing his business, he initiated talks about a new project.

Marianne's perceptive leadership proved that once team members were assigned to projects that suited them, they felt seen, heard, and valued. Her story highlights the importance of understanding diverse personalities and preferences, and demonstrates that a leader's ability to harness the needs, desires and motivations of their team members can yield astonishing results for both companies and individuals.

Leading multi-generational teams

As you develop your understanding of different personality types, it is crucial to acknowledge another facet of diversity: age. Workplaces are a mix of ages and generations. Since each generation has its own set of values, attitudes, and approach to work, leading a successful multi-generational team requires a collaborative and understanding culture. While a generational mix can result in a dynamic, multi-faceted environment, it can be challenging to manage wildly differing expectations, perspectives, and preferences. By understanding and valuing the unique attributes of each generation, leaders can create a more inclusive, productive, and satisfying work environment.

The five generations

The concept of generations begins with the Silent Generation, who were born after World War I, and came of age as increased mechanism changed the face of work. Five generations later, Gen Z, born around the turn of the millennium, face a future dominated by artificial intelligence and digital technology. Because Gen Z, Millennials, and Gen X make up the bulk of today's workforce, I start with the youngest generation (Gen Z) and work backwards down the decades. The timespan for each generation represents birth years. If we take 20 as an average age for entering the workplace, this means that, for example, the oldest Gen Zers, in their mid-twenties, probably have some work experience, whereas the youngest, who are still teenagers, are the employees of tomorrow.

Generation Z (1997–c.2010)

Gen Z (also known as Zoomers) is the cohort currently entering the workforce. Accustomed to rapid advances in technology, these digital natives take instant communication and high-speed connectivity for granted. Seldom parted from their devices (phones, tablets, smart watches, fitness trackers, etc.), they are social media-savvy, and tapped into current and emerging digital trends.

Global interconnectedness has given them a broad worldview, leading to an elevated social consciousness, and a desire to bring about political, societal and environmental change. However, they tend to be pragmatic and financially cautious.

The key to understanding Gen Z is acknowledging the socio-digital fabric that shapes them. Leaders wanting to unlock their potential must figure out how to harness their youthful enthusiasm, while addressing their concerns, and creating an environment that engages and challenges them.

STRENGTHS

- **Digital proficiency** Able to seamlessly navigate between platforms, devices, and digital tools.
- **Diverse and inclusive** Readily accepting of different cultures, identities, and perspectives.
- **Problem solvers** Growing up in a rapidly changing world, they've developed acute adaptability and problem-solving skills.
- **Socially conscious** Highly concerned with issues around social justice, equality, and the global environment, leading to a strong desire to make a positive impact.

POTENTIAL CHALLENGES

- **Short attention spans** Constant digital notifications and the speed of social media may result in reduced attention spans.
- **Over-reliance on technology** Being tech-savvy, they can lean too heavily on digital tools at the expense of tried and tested methods.
- **Need for instant gratification** Being accustomed to the immediacy of the digital world, they find it hard to exercise patience and persistence.
- **Mental health concerns** High incidence of anxiety and stress, partly due to societal and peer pressure, partly due to reliance on social media as a source of information.
- **High mobility and job-hopping** Eagerness for new experiences results in frequent job changes, or a preference for freelance or short-term contracts (gig economy). Companies may struggle to retain Gen Z employees who are not yet established in their careers.

> **Neuroscience insight**
>
> Because Gen Z brains have developed in a period of rapid information exchange, they have exceptional multi-modal processing capabilities. However, constant digital exposure has repercussions on their neural circuitry, impacting on their attention span and making them more susceptible to mental health problems. The neural reward pathways, notably those involving dopamine, are activated by regular interaction with digital platforms, which offer instant gratification.[5]

APPLICABLE LEADERSHIP STRATEGY

1. **Provide micro-learning opportunities** Due to their short attention spans, you may find that bite-sized learning modules can be more effective than prolonged sessions.
2. **Foster digital collaboration** Utilize their digital proficiency by incorporating the latest collaborative tools and platforms into their work.
3. **Support wellbeing initiatives** Encourage them to participate in wellbeing programs that address issues around stress and anxiety, and promote work-life balance.
4. **Offer real-world experiences** Opportunities for hands-on experience and/or internships will help to merge their digital know-how with real-world skills.
5. **Give regular feedback** Better than any generation, they appreciate a constant feedback loop to help them course-correct and move in the right direction.
6. **Incorporate social impact projects** Cater to their socially conscious mindset by aligning them with projects that have a social or environmental impact.
7. **Schedule digital detox periods** Remind them that occasional "digital detoxing" will boost their focus and mental wellbeing.
8. **Present opportunities for growth** Providing clarity on potential career development and personal advancement will help them visualize a future within the organization.

Millennials (1981–1996)

Born in an era of rapid technological advancement, Millennials (Gen Y) were the first cohort to grow up with the internet and mobile devices, and the first to which the term "digital native" fully applies. As forerunners of the digital revolution, they are pioneers of social media, the gig economy, and the digital nomad lifestyle. Millennials value meaningful work and a sense of purpose, and seek a collaborative work environment. Coming of age in a post 9/11 world, where global financial crises and political uncertainty are the norm, they tend to be skeptical of established systems and are not afraid to challenge the status quo.

Recognizing their strengths and challenges, and tailoring your leadership approach to cater to their unique needs, will not only improve team cohesion, but it will also tap into their potential for driving innovation and progress within the organization.

STRENGTHS

- **Technologically savvy** As digital natives, they are adept at navigating modern technologies and digital platforms.
- **Collaborative** They prefer a flat organizational structure, thrive in team environments, and value collaboration.
- **Adaptable** Accustomed to rapid changes in technology and society, they can adjust quickly to new ideas or strategies.
- **Purpose-driven** They seek roles that align with their personal values and offer a sense of purpose, not just a paycheck.

POTENTIAL CHALLENGES

- **Impatience** Having grown up in the age of instant gratification, they might seek rapid career progression or immediate results.
- **Perceived entitlement** They often have high expectations for their workplace, which can sometimes be interpreted as entitlement.
- **Job-hopping** In search of ideal conditions, or to align with personal values, they switch jobs more frequently than older generations.

Neuroscience insight

Constant exposure to digital stimuli has impacted the Millennial brain. Accustomed to having information always at their fingertips, their brains have developed exceptional multitasking capabilities. However, constant digital engagement might be linked to shorter attention spans. Constant surges of dopamine, a neurotransmitter associated with reward and pleasure, from social media notifications or rapid digital interactions, might explain their desire for frequent feedback.[6]

APPLICABLE LEADERSHIP STRATEGY

1. **Give continuous feedback** Instead of conducting annual reviews, schedule regular feedback sessions to support their need for consistent engagement and acknowledgment.
2. **Emphasize purpose over paycheck** They place a high value on their work having purpose or meaning, so try to give them projects that align with their values.
3. **Recognize their priorities** They favor a work-life blend over the traditional work-life balance, so offer opportunities for remote work, flexible hours, or sabbaticals, where possible.
4. **Provide opportunities for development** Because personal growth and professional development are equally important, provide opportunities for both skills development and emotional enhancement.
5. **Encourage collaboration** Utilize their natural tendency for working with others to build a workplace where teamwork and collaboration are encouraged.
6. **Be transparent** Because they appreciate open communication, be transparent about company decisions, goals and visions, and challenges.
7. **Offer mentoring programs** Pair them with mentors who can guide their career path, offer advice, and provide the feedback they crave.
8. **Create a diverse and inclusive culture** Promoting diversity and inclusivity within the workplace will align with their values and help to promote a sense of belonging.

Generation X (1965–1980)

Gen Xers were once regarded as the "middle child", lodged between the dominant presence of the Baby Boomers and the enthusiastic Millennials. This bridge generation grew up in an era of significant societal shifts, including a rise in divorce rates, and both parents working (they were the original latchkey kids). As the first cohort to fully embrace the personal computer, Generation X witnessed the evolution of new technology. Independent, resourceful, and self-sufficient, they tend to prefer a hands-off management style, and place significant importance on work-life balance.

Leading Gen Xers requires a nuanced approach. Their overall adaptability and balanced perspective make them invaluable in diverse teams, where they can help to bridge gaps and foster collaboration. Acknowledge their experience and point out opportunities for growth, especially for younger employees. Bear in mind that older Gen Xers, who are heading towards retirement from formal employment, may be seeking new opportunities and second careers in the informal (freelance) sector.

STRENGTHS

- **Technological adaptors** Gen Xers have been at the forefront of many technological advances and are comfortable navigating between analog and digital mediums.
- **Autonomous** Highly self-reliant and competent, they often thrive when given independence in their roles.
- **Balanced perspective** Having lived through major technological and societal changes, they bring a holistic view to projects and decisions.
- **Adaptable** Being accustomed to change, they can readily adjust to shifting circumstances.

POTENTIAL CHALLENGES

- **Seeking validation** Growing up in an era where their achievements were often overlooked in favor of their Boomer predecessors or Millennial successors, they can feel the need for regular affirmation or validation of their efforts.

- **Skepticism** They can be wary of new initiatives or strategies, stemming from their experiences during economic downturns, or situations such as the dot-com bubble burst of 2000. They may also fear the future impact of AI in the workplace.
- **Sandwiched responsibilities** They often bear responsibility for both older and younger generations in the workplace, as well as at home.

Neuroscience insight

Neuroplasticity is an indicator of how readily the brain adapts to change. As a group, this cohort assimilated technological change in different ways. Older Gen Xers first encountered technology in adulthood (transitioning from word processors to computer terminals), while younger members grew up with personal computers. Therefore, older Gen Xers may have undergone a conscious adaptation process, while younger ones integrated technological advances seamlessly during their formative years. The dynamic nature of neuroplasticity highlights Gen X's capacity to learn and adapt, making them adept at bridging traditional and modern practices.[7]

APPLICABLE LEADERSHIP STRATEGY

1. **Provide autonomy** Harness their independent nature by allowing them to take charge of projects, or define their roles, offering guidance only when necessary.
2. **Give regular feedback** Gen Xers value independence, but also like to know they are on the right track. Regular, constructive feedback can boost their confidence and drive.
3. **Encourage work-life balance** They place high importance on personal time, so provide opportunities for remote work and/or flexible hours.
4. **Offer opportunities for advancement** Encourage them to participate in workshops or training courses. (This may only apply to individuals who are still at a stage in their careers where upskilling or cross-skilling would be beneficial.)
5. **Include them in decision-making** Use strategic discussions or decision-making sessions to make the most of their balanced perspective and invaluable insights.

6. **Promote peer-to-peer collaboration** Encourage collaboration among team members, as well as with colleagues in other divisions. Don't overlook their potential to be mediators across generations; the ability to understand Boomers (their parents) and Millennials (their children) gives Gen X a unique perspective.

7. **Acknowledge their contributions** Recognizing specific achievements and contributions can address their need for validation.

8. **Provide challenges** The opportunity to take on a new challenge, or tackle a different role, can keep them engaged and motivated.

Baby Boomers (1946–1964)

Baby Boomers, or simply Boomers, grew up during a time of global prosperity, reform, and revolution. Born in the post-World War II era, they witnessed significant societal changes, from civil rights movements to the birth of rock 'n' roll. They ushered in an era of rapid economic growth, and are viewed as the generation that changed the world with their forward-thinking ideologies and trailblazing spirit. They were once a dominant presence in the workplace, but now that most of the cohort have reached retirement age, their influence is waning. However, it is worth remembering that many tech pioneers and innovators, including some who still drive the industry today, are Boomers!

If your team includes Boomers, you need to recognize their experience and work ethic. Harness their inherent team spirit to foster a harmonious and productive environment. If necessary, allow them more time to adopt tech-related changes.

STRENGTHS

- **Optimism** Generally, Boomers have a positive outlook towards work, often aiming for the betterment of the organization as a whole.
- **Team-oriented** Boomers are team players who value collaborative efforts and understand the importance of unity in achieving goals.
- **Strong work ethic** Raised in an era where reward was tied to effort, they're known for their dedication and commitment to their roles.

- **Relationship-focused** Personal relationships in the workplace matter, making them excellent at networking and building connections.

POTENTIAL CHALLENGES

- **Perception of technology** Although they witnessed the dawn of the digital age, they are not as tech-savvy as younger generations and may prefer older methods.
- **Work-life balance** Boomers often prioritize work over self, and they frequently downplay the importance of personal time, which can lead to burnout.
- **Change management** Having spent most of their working life in traditional business structures, they might find rapid organizational changes challenging.

Neuroscience insight

Baby Boomers have a wealth of experience and acquired knowledge. Cognitive flexibility, the ability to adapt to new situations or think about multiple concepts simultaneously, can be nurtured through continuous learning. Studies have shown that when the Boomer generation is introduced to new technologies or methods, they adapt quite efficiently, especially when they see the practical application of such changes.[8]

APPLICABLE LEADERSHIP STRATEGY

1. **Promote collaboration** Involve them in group projects or collaborative efforts. Their team-oriented nature and seasoned perspective can be invaluable in making decisions and implementing strategy.
2. **Recognize their experience** Encourage them to share their expertise and experience by conducting workshops or knowledge-sharing sessions. Acknowledging their achievements, both past and present, can enhance motivation.

3. **Provide learning opportunities** Training sessions will enhance skills and promote cognitive flexibility, especially if new digital tools or technology are involved.
4. **Give clear feedback** Because Boomers value both giving and receiving feedback, establish clear channels to ensure they remain aligned with organizational goals.
5. **Promote work-life balance** Offer flexible work hours and, where possible, opportunities for remote work.

Traditionalists (1925–1945)

Traditionalists, also known as the Silent Generation, grew up during periods of significant upheaval, including the Great Depression and World War II. These events shaped a generation that learned the values of sacrifice, frugality, and resilience. Their legendary work ethic came from being raised in an era where resources were scarce and hard work was the key to survival. Respect for authority and hierarchical structures, combined with a commitment to the organizations they served, made them foundational pillars of the mid-20th century workplace.

It is uncommon to still find members of this cohort in corporations, although they may remain involved in family businesses, or enterprises, such as charitable organizations, where their knowledge, expertise and commitment can be put to good use. If you have Traditionalists in your team, you need to strike a balance between honoring their experience, while integrating them into the evolving landscape of modern workplaces.

STRENGTHS

- **Loyalty and diligence** Their meticulous approach ensures that tasks are completed thoroughly.
- **Dependability** They will always ensure that projects are seen through to the very end.
- **Respect for hierarchy** They recognize organizational structures, and prefer clear roles and responsibilities.

POTENTIAL CHALLENGES

- **Resistance to change** They are unlikely to adapt readily to new technology or ways of doing things.
- **Communication styles** Preference for face-to-face conversations and "properly written" communications.
- **Hierarchical expectations** Belief in top-down management can inhibit open dialogue.

Neuroscience insight

The brain's plasticity (ability to adapt and change) decreases with age. However, this doesn't mean that older adults can't contribute. Neural networks established over decades allow them to draw on their experience to address present challenges, and they activate more brain regions when problem-solving than younger individuals. This makes them valuable sources of wisdom and insight.[9]

APPLICABLE LEADERSHIP STRATEGY

1. **Recognize their experience** Involving them in decision-making, strategizing or problem-solving not only gives you insight into past successes or challenges, it also offers a well-grounded perspective.
2. **Establish clear communication** Schedule regular check-ins to accommodate their preference for direct communication. Feedback that is structured and clear will help them take effective action.
3. **Encourage knowledge sharing** Providing opportunities to share their experience and anecdotes preserves vital institutional knowledge that may inform future decisions.
4. **Offer personalized training** One-on-one training sessions will help them adapt to new tools or methods.

The benefits of leading a diverse team

Diverse teams can benefit from the range of ideas, perspectives and approaches that each individual contributes. Diversity goes beyond age, gender, or ethnic background to encompass experience, skill, and character. Leveraging diversity can encourage innovative thinking, and improve a team's ability to solve problems. A study by Larson (2017) found that diverse teams make better decisions up to 87 percent of the time.[10]

However, the benefits of diversity can only be realized in an environment that is inclusive and respectful, and where every voice is heard and valued. This includes the sharing of ideas, giving credit where it is due, and facilitating open discussion.

Good leadership goes beyond hitting targets and boosting the company's balance sheet. It is about promoting an organizational culture that encourages everyone to feel part of the collective whole. As a leader, your role in shaping this culture cannot be overstated. Respecting all team members, listening with empathy, recognizing individual contributions, and adapting your leadership style as necessary, can go a long way towards building an inclusive culture.

... the benefits of diversity can only be realized in an environment that is inclusive and respectful, and where every voice is heard and valued.

Leading a diverse team is a process of developing and maintaining a culture where learning and growth are valued, and individuals feel safe to express their ideas. Successful leaders know how to integrate different generations into a harmonious team. The bonus is that understanding your team members may help you to understand yourself better.

SELF-REFLECTION PIT STOP

Scan the QR code or visit drtomdreyer.com/tools to download your e-toolkit.

Understanding your team

1. **Personality assessment models**
   1. Have you used personality assessment models to help you understand your team better? If yes, what was the experience like? If no, could using assessment models enhance your understanding of individual team members?
   2. Based on the assessment models, reflect on how many different personality types you have in your team, and how these differences may have influenced team dynamics.

2. **Leadership personality**
   1. After reviewing the MBTI, DISC, Enneagram, and CLPS models, consider your own leadership personality. Which model do you feel best captures this, and why?
   2. Have you adapted your leadership approach to accommodate different personality types? Are there areas where you could improve?

3. **Strategies for using personality assessment models**
   1. Reflect on areas such as communication, conflicts, or personal development that can be addressed using personality assessment models. If you have used these to resolve issues in the past, how did they affect your team dynamics?
   2. Can you identify any situations where using personality assessment models could have improved the outcome?

4. **Leading a multi-generational team**
   1. Reflect on your experiences of leading a multi-generational team. What challenges or opportunities have arisen?
   2. Is there anything you could do to improve your leadership of a multi-generational team?

5. Inclusion and diversity

1. What strategies do you use to create an inclusive and diverse environment within your team?
2. Are there any areas related to inclusion and diversity where you could improve?

6. Set SMART goals

Based on your reflections, set 2–3 SMART goals to enhance your understanding and leadership of different personality types. For example, if you identified that you need to work on leading a multi-generational team, a SMART goal could be: "In the next month, I will implement one new strategy to improve communication between the different generations in my team."

Effective leaders appreciate diversity, and adapt their leadership style to cater for multiple personality types and generations within their team. Recognizing that we are all different enables you to appreciate the individuality of your team members. Personality assessments can provide useful insights into the values that drive individual behaviors, and equip you with a way to express and discuss differences. Just remember that assessment models are not intended to put people into boxes; rather use them to highlight the unique strengths and attributes of individual team members.

Revisit your reflections and goals regularly to track your progress and make adjustments. The power to lead successfully lies within your grasp.

... assessment models are not intended to put people into boxes; rather use them to highlight the unique strengths and attributes of individual team members.

Endnotes

1   Depue, R. A., & Collins, P. F. (1999). Neurobiology of the structure of personality: Dopamine, facilitation of incentive motivation, and extraversion. *Behavioral and Brain Sciences*, 22(3), 491-517.

2   Nielsen, J. A., Zielinski, B. A., Ferguson, M. A., Lainhart, J. E., & Anderson, J. S. (2013). An evaluation of the left-brain vs. right-brain hypothesis with resting state functional connectivity magnetic resonance imaging. *PLoS One*, 8(8), e71275.

3   Amodio, D. M., & Frith, C. D. (2006). Meeting of minds: the medial frontal cortex and social cognition. *Nature Reviews Neuroscience*, 7(4), 268-277.
    Kosfeld, M., Heinrichs, M., Zak, P. J., Fischbacher, U., & Fehr, E. (2005). Oxytocin increases trust in humans. *Nature*, 435(7042), 673-676.
    LeDoux, J. (2007). The amygdala. *Current Biology*, 17(20), R868-R874.

4   Adcock, R. A., Thangavel, A., Whitfield-Gabrieli, S., Knutson, B., & Gabrieli, J. D. E. (2006). Reward-motivated learning: Mesolimbic activation precedes memory formation. *Neuron*, 50(3), 507-517.
    Baumgartner, T., Heinrichs, M., Vonlanthen, A., Fischbacher, U., & Fehr, E. (2008). Oxytocin shapes the neural circuitry of trust and trust adaptation in humans. *Neuron*, 58(4), 639-650.
    Mehta, P. H., & Josephs, R. A. (2010). Testosterone and cortisol jointly regulate dominance: Evidence for a dual-hormone hypothesis. *Hormones and Behavior*, 58(5), 898-906.

5   Zhou, Y., Li, Y., Yang, J., Yang, M., & Guo, Q. (2023). Impact of digital media use on the developing brain: A systematic review and meta-analysis. *Frontiers in Human Neuroscience*, 17.

6   Gazzaley, A., Rosen, L. D., Behroozi, M. M., & Kramer, D. R. (2021). Attention span, distractibility, and the impact of digital media on young adults. *Psychological Science*, 32(9), 1453-1463.

7   Spreng, R. N., & Turner, G. R. (2019). The shifting architecture of cognition and brain function in older adulthood. *Perspectives on Psychological Science*, 14(4), 523-542.

8   Padmanabhan, K., Kramer, D. R., Moffat, S. D., Thompson, N. S., & Gutchess, A. (2023). Cognitive flexibility in older adults: Exploring the mediating role of executive function and novelty seeking. *Neuropsychologia*, 184, 107960.

9   Cabeza, R., Albert, M., Belleville, S., Craik, F. I. M., Duarte, A., Grady, C. L., Lindenberger, U., Nyberg, L., Park, D. C., Reuter-Lorenz, P. A., Rugg, M. D., Steffener, J., & Rajah, M. N. (2018). Maintenance, reserve and compensation: the cognitive neuroscience of healthy ageing. *Nature Reviews Neuroscience*, 19(11), 701-710.

10 Larson, E. (2017, September 19). Infographic: Diversity + Inclusion = Better Decision Making At Work. Cloverpop. Retrieved from https://www.cloverpop.com/blog/infographic-diversity-inclusion-better-decision-making-at-work

GOLDEN STAR

BUILDING TRUST

Golden Star 4 examines the role of trust in leadership, from establishing the cycle of trust to applying the Trust-to-Results pyramid. You will learn how to build trust and maintain it in a manner that deepens your connection with team members and strengthens your leadership practice.

What is trust?

The concept of trust has been explored by numerous writers, theorists, and thinkers, each of whom brings their unique perspective and insights. Let's look at what they have to say.

Barbara Brooks Kimmel, CEO of Trust Across America–Trust Around the World, suggests that trust is a function of credibility, integrity, and authenticity. According to Kimmel, **credibility** means being reliable, and having the necessary expertise for a role; **integrity** embodies honesty and maintaining strong moral principles; and **authenticity** is about being genuine in one's actions and words.

Psychologist, scientist, and author Robert Plutchik views trust from an emotional and evolutionary perspective, identifying it as comprising elements of anticipation, acceptance, and fear. For Plutchik, trusting someone involves the **anticipation** of a positive outcome, **acceptance** of the individual's behavior, and an inherent **fear** of the risks involved. While this may be a less-traditional view, it underlines both the complexity and the emotional nature of trust.

In *The Thin Book of Trust: An Essential Primer for Building Trust at Work*, Charles Feltman describes trust as a combination of **sincerity**, **reliability**, and **competence**, with the added factor of care. He argues that true trust can only be established when a leader demonstrates care for their team members' interests, and wellbeing beyond just their work.

In a more business-oriented view, David Maister, Charles Green, and Robert Galford, co-authors of *The Trusted Advisor*, propose a trust equation: Trustworthiness equals credibility plus reliability plus intimacy, all divided by self-orientation. In this equation, **credibility** is about your words being dependable, **reliability** concerns consistent behavior over time, **intimacy** is about safety in discussions, and **self-orientation** is about the focus being on the other person, not yourself.

Business consultant, Ken Blanchard, describes trust as a function of both character and competence. **Character** involves your values, principles, and behavior, while **competence** includes your skills and abilities. According to Blanchard, leaders can only gain trust when they display both high character and high competence.

So, we have different perspectives, each with their unique equation, but what do they all boil down to?

At its core, trust is about credibility, authenticity, care, emotional safety, and low self-orientation. It's about both your character, which includes your integrity and sincerity, and your competence, which incorporates your skills and reliability.

Yet, trust isn't static; it is a continuum that needs to be nurtured; an ongoing process that requires a leader to consistently demonstrate these values and behaviors. As Stephen M.R. Covey says in *The Speed of Trust*, "Trust is the one thing that changes everything".

In leadership, trust is not just a nice-to-have, it is a must-have. It is the unseen force that holds organizations together and serves as the foundation for high-performing teams. Without trust, leadership is merely a hollow title.

Picture a leader standing in front of a team to announce a major decision. If the leader has built a degree of trust, the team members are likely to accept the decision, even if it is a tough one. They will believe the leader has their best interests at heart and has made a well-informed choice. But what if the leader hasn't established trust? Then, resistance, skepticism, and discord are likely outcomes. It's like trying to drive a car with the handbrake on; it's hard to get anywhere, and you're causing damage all the way.

In *The Leadership Challenge*, Jim Kouzes and Barry Posner write: "The first law of leadership: If you don't believe in the messenger, you won't believe the message." This underscores how vital trust is in leadership, supported by neuroscience insights. So, how can leaders build this trust?

How trust shapes the brain

Neuroscience has begun to unravel how trust shapes our brain, and influences everything from the way we interact with others, to how we innovate, to levels of resilience in leadership.[1] Trust is not just a moral attribute but a neurobiological agent that shapes cooperation, innovation, communication, and resilience in profound ways. The neuroscience of trust provides a compelling way to help us understand effective leadership.

1. **Trust and cooperation: The oxytocin connection**

   When it comes to team dynamics, the interplay between trust and cooperation is deeply neurobiological. Oxytocin, often dubbed the "social hormone", is pivotal here. A study by Kosfeld, Heinrichs, Zak, Fischbacher, and Fehr (2005)[2] revealed that elevated levels of oxytocin enhance trust which, in turn, fosters cooperative behavior. This hormonal shift makes team members feel secure and valued which, in turn, encourages them to collaborate and share ideas. In such an environment, the brain's defense mechanisms, like fear of criticism, are lowered, leading to more cohesive and effective teamwork.

2. **Trust as a brain reward: Heightened engagement and productivity**

   Trust activates the brain's reward circuits, notably those linked to the ventromedial prefrontal cortex. A study by Zink et al. (2008)[3] showed that when an individual perceives trustworthiness in others, their brain's reward system lights up. This neurobiological response translates to heightened engagement and productivity in the workplace. For employees, feeling trusted acts as a neural reward, motivating them to invest more passion and effort into their work.

3. **Trust and innovation: The role of the amygdala**

   The amygdala is the brain's center for fear and risk evaluation. A study by Lennartsson et al. (2016)[4] found that high levels of trust reduce activity in the amygdala. This helps us overcome fear of failure, and promotes risk-taking, a mindset that is essential for innovation. In a trusting environment, the brain's instinctively wary response to new challenges diminishes, enabling individuals to propose creative solutions or embrace unfamiliar approaches without undue stress.

4. **Trust and the prefrontal cortex: Enhancing communication**

   Trust enhances communication by influencing the prefrontal cortex, which is responsible for decision-making and social interactions.

Eisenberger and Cole (2012)[5] show that social pain and pleasure are processed in the same brain regions as physical pain and pleasure. When trust is present, it mitigates social anxieties, enabling leaders and team members to communicate more openly and effectively.

5. **Trust and neuroplasticity: Building resilient teams**

   Trust fosters resilience, especially in challenging times. The brain's neuroplasticity is enhanced in a trusting environment. Davidson and McEwen (2012)[6] point out that when supportive social environments are underpinned by trust, it promotes neuroplasticity. This, in turn, helps individuals and teams to overcome adversity, and recover from setbacks more effectively.

6. **Trust and neural alignment: The synchronicity of minds**

   Recent studies suggest that trust plays a role in aligning the neural patterns of leaders and team members. Jiang et al. (2020)[7] discovered that during successful cooperative interactions, the brainwaves of the participants begin to synchronize. This neural alignment, facilitated by trust, promotes understanding and harmony within teams, and enhances collective problem-solving and decision-making.

Understanding the cycle of trust

Trust binds teams together, shapes their dynamics, and gives meaning to their collective efforts. To sustain trust, it must be constantly nurtured, sometimes jeopardized, and often rebuilt. Understanding this will help team members withstand pressure and overcome challenges.

The cycle of trust

- **Seeding** Building trust frequently begins with small gestures, such as a kept promise, positive feedback, or acknowledging a team member's value. Like planting a seed, this initial, or embryonic, stage is delicate and requires nurturing.

- **Nurturing** Once seeded, trust needs to be nurtured. This can be through regular acts of reliability, open dialogue, or authentic gestures of care and concern. It is akin to watering a plant, ensuring it gets enough sunlight, and protecting it from pests.
- **Blossoming** With consistent nurturing, trust blooms. It manifests in more robust collaborations, fewer hesitations, and a palpable sense of unity within the team. Decisions are made faster, and there is an implicit understanding that every team member is working with the best intentions.
- **Weathering challenges** No journey is without its challenges. The most trust-rich environments can face periods of doubt, brought on by unforeseen circumstances, miscommunications, or human errors. During such times, the foundations of earlier trust are often tested.
- **Rebuilding** Even if trust has been broken, it can be restored. This may require honest acknowledgment of mistakes, candid conversations and, perhaps most importantly, time to regroup, but the silver lining is that once trust is rebuilt, the relationship often emerges stronger for having overcome the challenges.

The dynamics of trust

Once you understand the cycle of trust, you can begin to grasp the dynamics that play out on both sides of the trust equation.

- **Admit vulnerability** Trust involves a degree of vulnerability. Whether it is a leader admitting they don't have all the answers, or a team member voicing a concern, trust is built when individuals have the courage to admit their vulnerability.
- **Be reliable** Trust develops in the presence of reliability. Behaving or acting the same way time after time makes you appear to be both reliable and trustworthy.
- **Give feedback** Within the trust cycle, feedback serves as a vital tool. Leaders can use feedback from team members to understand how they are perceived, and what they can do to strengthen their bonds of trust.

- **Practice empathy** Every individual has a sense of what trust means to them, and which behaviors or actions make them feel valued and safe. For some, it might be recognition or acknowledgement, for others, autonomy or inclusivity. Being empathic towards these nuances helps leaders build trust with their team members.

Techniques for establishing trust and credibility

Building trust and credibility is a slow process that requires consistency. Leaders who build trust with their teams unlock tremendous potential for individual growth, innovation, and achievement. Practical techniques to establish trust and credibility include that the leader should:

1. **Display honesty and integrity** Trust begins with personal honesty and integrity. This entails always telling the truth, even when it is difficult, and acting ethically, even when nobody's watching. Honest leaders are trusted because they are not afraid to admit their mistakes, or accept responsibility for their actions.
2. **Be consistent** Consistency in words and actions is important for building trust. By being consistent, leaders demonstrate predictability. And, because predictability fosters a sense of security and trust, their team members know what to expect.
3. **Demonstrate competence** Leaders who are competent instill confidence in their team. Competence goes beyond just being good at a job, or having the appropriate knowledge or skills. It involves understanding the business or industry you are in, knowing its challenges and trends, making informed decisions, and providing guidance to others.
4. **Show concern** Leaders who genuinely care for their people earn their trust. This means taking an interest in other people's lives, listening to their concerns, helping them overcome challenges, and celebrating their successes.
5. **Communicate effectively** Open, or two-way, communication fosters trust. Leaders should talk with team members, listen to what they have to say, and be willing to discuss difficult topics. Open communication shows that you have nothing to hide, and this builds credibility.

6. **Follow through on commitments** Trust is broken when leaders fail to keep their promises. Leaders should be careful about making commitments because, once a commitment has been made, they must do everything possible to follow through.

7. **Lead by example** Show team members that you are not just talk, but that you can also take action when circumstances demand it. Leaders who "walk their talk" earn the respect and trust of their team.

8. **Foster an inclusive environment** Trust flourishes in safe environments. Leaders can cultivate this by embracing diversity, promoting inclusivity, and encouraging everyone to voice their opinions and ideas.

9. **Be humble** Humility is a powerful trust-building attribute. Leaders who are humble accept their limitations, are open to feedback, and are not afraid to ask for help. They understand that they don't have all the answers, and this vulnerability helps build trust.

10. **Show resilience** Leaders who show resilience in the face of adversity earn the trust of their teams. Resilience includes remaining calm in a crisis, maintaining a positive attitude even under pressure, and believing in their vision and strategy.

Former US Secretary of State, Colin Powell once said, "Trust is the glue that holds people together, and the lubricant that keeps an organization moving forward." Using the techniques outlined here, leaders can build an environment of trust, and establish a team that is both loyal and capable of producing exceptional results.

The Trust-to-Results Pyramid

The Trust-to-Results Pyramid illustrates the journey from basic trust to tangible results. It shows how relationships that are built on trust present opportunities, drive action, and lead to remarkable outcomes.

TRUST-TO-RESULTS PYRAMID

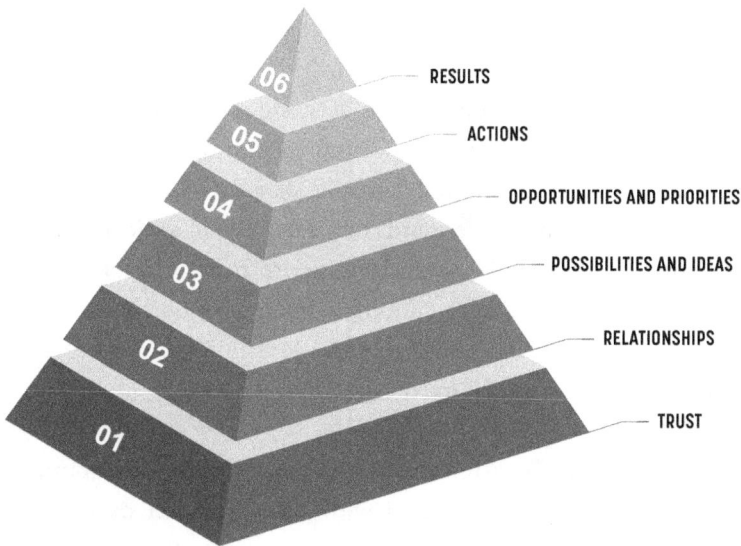

1. **Trust** Anchored by values such as honesty, dependability, and competence, trust is the foundation upon which all the other levels rest. As a leader, establishing trust sets the tone for the leader-follower relationship and creates a strong base for all subsequent interactions.

2. **Relationships** We build relationships on the bedrock of trust. Effective leaders recognize team members as individuals, acknowledge their strengths, motivate them through their interests, and support them to overcome their weaknesses. This tier is about developing interpersonal connectivity, mutual respect, and the leader's commitment to their team.

3. **Possibilities and ideas** Good relationships provide a solid platform for dialogue and the free exchange of ideas. Use the power of collective thinking to unlock possibilities and spark fresh ideas. Trust opens up a space where creativity thrives, innovation is encouraged, and diverse perspectives are welcomed.

4. **Opportunities and priorities** Leaders must identify opportunities, investigate promising prospects, and prioritize them according to how they align with the team's goals. It is at this stage that vision takes shape and strategic direction is formulated.

5. **Actions** Once opportunities have been identified and priorities set, it is time to act. Actions turn opportunities into reality. Effective leaders foster a sense of commitment to the shared vision, and ensure that every team member understands his or her role in achieving it.

6. **Results** The pyramid's pinnacle is where trust, relationships, ideas, opportunities, and actions culminate in tangible outcomes, or results. On reaching this tier, leaders can measure their team's performance and see the fruits of their collective labor.

Leaders can use the Trust-to-Results Pyramid to illustrate a journey that begins with basic trust, and ends with the realization of results. This progression demonstrates how trust connects different aspects of leadership, and holds the key to successful outcomes.

STORY IN PRACTICE

Build trust before building a team

When John Taylor, an experienced team leader in the energy industry, accepted a position in Abu Dhabi, he was excited about moving to another country, and taking on a new challenge. Despite knowing that the company had fired two previous people in his position for poor results, he was confident he could turn around the performance of the team.

In his first week on the job, John met with his deputies. One-by-one, they filed into his office to welcome him, but offered little explanation for the team's poor results. Some blamed the environment, or employees who were not as productive as they could be, others blamed the strategy, and so on. Later in the week, it was the turn of Anthony Smith, an experienced field engineer. He was not what John expected. A giant of a man, with a bushy beard, walked in, sat down opposite John, and said nothing. John began his usual greeting. "Anthony, I look forward...". "Call me Tony," he interrupted.

"Tony," said John, "I look forward to working with you and the team..." As John talked, Tony did not move, not even the occasional nod of the head. "I'm not here to change things for the sake of change," John continued. "I'm here to do everything I can to support our success." He ended his speech as usual: "Is there anything I need to know to help me help you in your job?" Tony looked him in the eye, and decided to take a chance. "John," he said, "We've seen bosses come and go. Like you, they start off with a nice speech, but then do very little to help us do our jobs properly. To be frank, John, many of us are wondering: Why should we trust you?"

John began to understand why, despite the undeniable potential of his team, they were falling short. Further meetings confirmed his sentiments. Morale was at rock bottom, productivity was suffering, and team cohesion was visibly lacking.

Clearly, something had to change, and it had to start with him. Recognizing the role that trust plays in effective leadership, John set out to prove his credibility. He organized a series of town-hall meetings where he invited everyone to discuss the obstacles the team faced. John shared his strategic vision, speaking candidly about the challenge of not repeating his predecessors' mistakes. He outlined his turnaround plans, and expressed a commitment to transparency at all levels. Slowly, his words began to sow the seeds of trust among his sceptical team leaders.

Knowing that trust is built over time, John made consistency a key strategy in his approach. To ensure his actions mirrored his words, he refrained from making promises he couldn't keep.

John took the initiative to form a working relationship with every person on his team. Because he wanted the relationships to be authentic, he proceeded at a pace that he felt was right for each individual. Some were immediately receptive to his interest in them; others took a wait-and-see approach, and that was fine. He believed that, over time, even the wariest team members would recognize his sincerity. And he was right. By trying to understand their apprehensions and aspirations, celebrating their achievements, providing support if it was required, and genuinely caring about their wellbeing, John fostered a sense of mutual respect and belonging that significantly improved team dynamics.

As he built a solid foundation of trust, and established authentic, open relationships with his team, the other levels of the Trust-to-Results Pyramid started to fall into place.

Recognizing that an innovative environment was critical for growth, John encouraged his team to explore all possibilities. This generated a flurry of new ideas that unlocked fresh opportunities. John aligned these opportunities with the team's goals. By ensuring that every team member had a clear understanding of their role, he established a shared sense of responsibility and purpose.

The transformed team showed renewed dedication and enthusiasm as they worked together to meet their goals. Levels of engagement soared, innovative solutions resolved old problems, and productivity increased. Within two years, John's team exceeded its targets, earning recognition as one of the company's high-performing teams.

John Taylor's story illustrates the positive impact of relationships built on trust. By placing trust at the core of his approach, he transformed a struggling team into one that was highly motivated, and united behind a common purpose. His journey underscores Stephen M.R. Covey's insight that "trust is the one thing that changes everything."

SELF-REFLECTION PIT STOP

Scan the QR code or visit drtomdreyer.com/tools to download your e-toolkit.

Trust

Building trust with others is a foundation of effective leadership. It is a continuous process, so revisit these reflections and goals regularly to track your progress.

1. **Foundations of trust**
   1. Credibility, authenticity, emotional safety, personal reputation, and workplace competence are all components of trust. Which applies most to you? Why?
   2. Which components could you could improve? How could you work on these areas to build greater trust with your team?

2. Understanding trust in leadership

1. Reflect on your understanding of trust in leadership prior to reading this Golden Star. Has your perspective changed after exploring the different facets of trust?
2. Can you identify instances where trust, or a lack thereof, significantly impacted your team's dynamics and performance?

3. The role of trust in teams

1. Reflect on how trust, or lack of it, has impacted your team. Consider things like cooperation, innovation, communication, and resilience; are there any incidents that stand out?
2. If trust has been lacking, what actions could you take to improve it?

4. Techniques for establishing trust

1. Do you use any of the techniques discussed in this Golden Star to establish trust and credibility, and enhance your leadership style?
2. If not, what can you do to incorporate these techniques into your leadership practice?

5. The Trust-to-Results Pyramid

1. After reviewing the Trust-to-Results Pyramid, can you identify instances when trust has influenced relationships, opened up possibilities, created opportunities, or yielded results for your team?
2. Are there any levels of the pyramid where you could improve? What actions could you take to enhance trust at these levels?

6. Promoting trust in relationships

1. Do you cultivate and maintain trustworthy relationships with your team members? Which strategies have been effective, and where could improvements be made?
2. Reflect on how a heightened focus on trust could impact your team's performance.

7. Set SMART goals

Set 2–3 SMART goals to strengthen the levels of trust within your team. For example, if you feel that you are not always consistent, a goal could be: "Over the next three months, I will use feedback from my team to identify areas where I could be more consistent in what I say and do."

Trust is a key component of leadership. This Golden Star explored how relationships built on trust can unlock potential, and how consistently applying the principles of trust boosts morale and improves productivity in individuals and teams.

Endnotes

1   Li, H., Liu, Y., Liu, J., Liu, X., Xu, H., & Yang, X. (2023). Leadership styles, neural processing, and employee creativity: A functional magnetic resonance imaging study. *Nature Neuroscience*, 26(10), 1380-1389.
     Wang, Y., Li, J., Zhou, B., & Yang, X. (2023). The neural underpinnings of leadership-induced resilience: A resting-state fMRI study. *Social Cognitive and Affective Neuroscience*, 18(9), 1977-1987.

2   Kosfeld, M., Heinrichs, M., Zak, P. J., Fischbacher, U., & Fehr, E. (2005). Oxytocin increases trust in humans. *Nature*, 435(7042), 673-676.

3   Zink, C. F., Tong, Y., Chen, Q., Bassett, D. S., Stein, J. L., & Meyer-Lindenberg, A. (2008). Know your place: Neural processing of social hierarchy in humans. *Neuron*, 58(2), 273-283.

4   Lennartsson, A. K., Kushnir, M. M., Bergquist, J., Jonsdottir, I. H., & Olsson, T. (2016). Sex steroid levels temporarily increase in response to acute psychosocial stress in healthy men and women. *International Journal of Psychophysiology*, 110, 39-46.

5   Eisenberger, N. I., & Cole, S. W. (2012). Social neuroscience and health: Neurophysiological mechanisms linking social ties with physical health. *Nature Neuroscience*, 15(5), 669-674.

6   Davidson, R. J., & McEwen, B. S. (2012). Social influences on neuroplasticity: Stress and interventions to promote well-being. *Nature Neuroscience*, 15(5), 689-695.

7   Jiang, J., Chen, C., Dai, B., Shi, G., Ding, G., Liu, L., & Lu, C. (2020). Leader emergence through interpersonal neural synchronization. *Proceedings of the National Academy of Sciences*, 117(14), 7564-7569.

GOLDEN STAR

DEVELOPING HIGH-PERFORMANCE TEAMS

Developing high-performance teams plays a crucial role in an organization's success. Renowned anthropologist, Margaret Mead, said, "Never doubt that a small group of thoughtful, committed citizens can change the world; indeed, it is the only thing that ever has." This statement carries weight when it comes to building a motivated and engaged team. When you integrate the principles of trust (Golden Star 4), with the development strategies presented in this Golden Star, you will lay the foundation for effectively leading a high-performance team.

The development of a high-performance team requires ongoing assessment to ensure that opportunities for individual development align with the team's goals and objectives. Golden Star 5 examines six models for assessing team performance: Tuckman's Five Stages of Team Development; the EACH Mindset Model; my own SPARKLE model; Maslow's Hierarchy of Needs; the GRPI model, and the Belbin Team Inventory.

Tuckman's Five Stages of Team Development

Leading a successful team can be likened to conducting a choir; it involves meticulous planning, managing a diverse range of talents, and maintaining harmony. And just like any good choir, most high-performing teams go through distinct stages of development. In 1965, American psychologist Bruce Tuckman introduced a five-stage model: Forming, Storming, Norming, Performing, and Adjourning. Let's examine what a proficient leader should do during each stage.

1. **Forming** At the initial stage, a team is a collection of individuals. The members are typically polite, excited, yet uncertain about the team's direction and their individual roles. As a leader, you need to bring everyone together, like the choirmaster during the first rehearsal. Here are the key steps you should take:
   - **Set direction** Define the team's purpose, mission, and goals. This provides a shared vision that everyone can align with.
   - **Create structure** Outline specific roles and responsibilities for each team member. This provides a clear path, allowing everyone to contribute meaningfully.

- **Foster a sense of belonging** Encourage team members to get to know one another by sharing their insights, hopes, and concerns. This will cultivate personal connections and build a team culture.

2. **Storming** This is often the most challenging stage, as it is when team members begin to express their individual perspectives, and disagreements may arise. It's like the interpretation of a piece of music where the individual parts are yet to be synchronized. As a leader, your role is to be the mediator.
   - **Refocus goals** Remind the team of their common goal. This helps to shift the focus away from disagreements or personal opinions, and towards shared objectives.
   - **Establish team processes** Define effective processes for decision-making, conflict resolution, and communication. This ensures that everyone's voice is heard, and makes provision for conflicts to be constructively managed.
   - **Formulate plans** Develop action plans with clear timelines, roles, and deliverables. This provides a road map for the team to follow.

3. **Norming** As the team finds its rhythm, members begin to appreciate each other's strengths, and discover their shared norms. This equates to the choir starting to sing in harmony. The leader's role is to keep the momentum going.
   - **Maintain focus** Encourage team members to remain focused on their shared goals and objectives, and discourage distractions.
   - **Encourage participation** Promote an open, inclusive environment where everyone feels comfortable expressing their ideas, as well as any concerns.
   - **Facilitate discussions** By fostering an atmosphere of mutual respect and understanding, you can ensure that all perspectives are heard, and differences are discussed openly.

4. **Performing** By this stage, the team should function like a well-tuned unit, with everyone working towards the same goal. Your role as a leader is to sustain this.

- **Provide feedback** Use regular communications to recognize achievements, indicate areas that may require improvement, and remind everyone of the progress that has been made.
- **Maintain processes** Ensure established processes are followed, and address any issues that might hinder the team's performance.
- **Celebrate** Acknowledge accomplishments and celebrate milestones. This boosts morale and motivates every team member to maintain their high performance levels.

5. **Adjourning** As the project or task comes to an end, and the team prepares to disband, your role is to provide closure. Think of this as the curtain call at a choral concert, where individuals are recognized for their contribution.
   - **Positive reinforcement** Acknowledge individual efforts, provide constructive feedback to the team as a whole, and express your gratitude for their hard work.
   - **Provide clear instructions** Ensure that any pending tasks are clearly assigned, and that all team members are aware of their post-project responsibilities.
   - **Prepare for the future** Discuss any upcoming projects or potential opportunities for the team to collaborate again.

Remember, a team seldom progresses through these stages in a linear manner. The team may cycle back to an earlier stage when new members join, or if they face unforeseen challenges. However, by understanding the stages, and the leader's role in each, you'll be well-equipped to guide your team through every eventuality.

EACH Mindset Model

A successful team leader plays a number of roles, from visionary to mediator, facilitator, coach, or mentor, depending on the needs of their team members at that moment. To switch seamlessly between roles, a leader needs to remain adaptable. British leadership coach and author Susanne Madsen favors the EACH Mindset Model as a self-analysis tool for objectively evaluating your leadership style. Based on four pillars:

Empowerment, Accountability, Courage, and Humility, it provides a starting point for understanding where you are now, and identifying what steps you can take to improve your own leadership and, consequently, your team's performance.

1. **Empowerment: Inspiring active participation**

   Empowerment fosters a sense of inclusion by encouraging team members to participate fully, and contribute their insights to the project. Empowered individuals develop an emotional investment in the team's objectives. Leaders can enhance this by creating an environment where individuals become part of a cohesive team, and feel valued and heard.

   "As a leader, I enable my team members to develop and excel by asking big things of them. I involve them in decision-making, I value their contributions, and I connect their work to the broad goals of the team."

2. **Accountability: Cultivating a sense of ownership**

   Accountability is about taking ownership. High-performance teams are marked by members who take responsibility for their actions, and own the results they produce. Good leaders know that accountability isn't about casting blame if things go wrong; it is about creating a culture where everyone feels responsible for the team's success.

   "I demonstrate confidence in my team members by holding them responsible for their promises. I set clear expectations, communicate these effectively, and follow up consistently."

3. **Courage: Taking risks**

   Courage involves the willingness to take calculated risks, express divergent opinions, challenge the status quo, and make tough decisions when necessary. When you lead by example, and create a safe space for open communication, team members will be more willing to step out of their comfort zones.

   "I am willing to set aside personal interests to achieve what needs to be done. I act on sound values and behavioral expectations, promote open dialogue, encourage innovative thinking, stand up for my team, and take responsibility for my decisions."

4. **Humility: The power of authentic leadership**

   Humility is a critical, but often-overlooked, quality in leadership. In a team context, it means that leaders recognize they don't have all the answers and are open to learning from others. By demonstrating humility, leaders show that they value the collective wisdom of the team above their personal egos.

   "I admit mistakes. I accept and learn from feedback. I seek different points of view and value the contributions of every team member."

EACH MINDSET MODEL

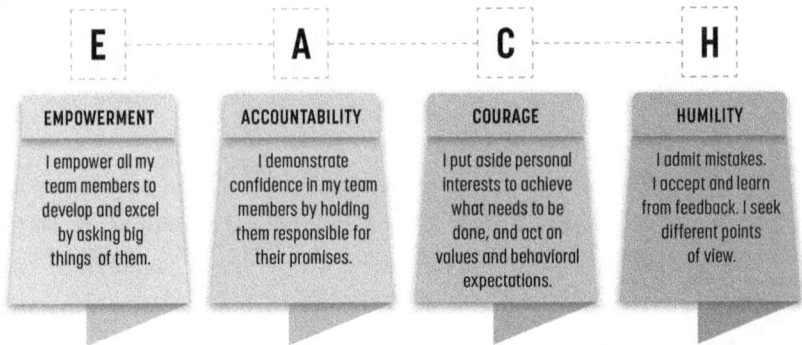

E	A	C	H
EMPOWERMENT	**ACCOUNTABILITY**	**COURAGE**	**HUMILITY**
I empower all my team members to develop and excel by asking big things of them.	I demonstrate confidence in my team members by holding them responsible for their promises.	I put aside personal interests to achieve what needs to be done, and act on values and behavioral expectations.	I admit mistakes. I accept and learn from feedback. I seek different points of view.

Applying the EACH Mindset Model

Developing a high-performance team requires introspection. Taking time to understand your personal strengths and weaknesses, and identifying areas for improvement, will help you make strategic decisions about your leadership style. By integrating the four pillars into your regular interactions and team development strategies, you will be ready to steer your team towards excellence. Just bear in mind that every member of a high-performance team is on their own journey of learning and improvement. Use the following questions to facilitate self-analysis, but remember that the goal is progress, not perfection.

Empowerment: Do I foster active participation?

- Do I engage with my team members, and take the time to understand their opinions and perspectives?
- Do I listen to how they might feel about a particular issue?
- Am I sensitive to cultural or language differences that might affect how my team members communicate?
- Do I provide constructive feedback that helps team members grow professionally?

Accountability: Do I cultivate a sense of ownership?

- Do I promote a culture of accountability by holding myself, as well as my team members, accountable for our words and actions?
- Do I ensure that everyone is held to the same standards of behavior and performance?
- Do I take responsibility for my own mistakes, and address any negative or exclusionary behavior?
- Are there steps I can take to ensure that tasks and projects are completed to the best of my team's ability?

Courage: Do I put personal interests aside for the sake of the team?

- Do I inspire my team members by taking risks, or fighting for things that will help us to get the job done?
- Do I recognize when team members are going through difficult times and offer support and understanding?
- Am I patient and understanding if someone makes a mistake, or fails to meet expectations?
- How can I create a safe space for team members to voice their opinions and challenge the status quo?

Humility: Am I able to accept mistakes and learn from them?

- Do I take responsibility for my team's successes and failures?
- Do I ensure that all team members feel valued and appreciated for their contributions?

- Do I show respect towards all my team members, regardless of their background or experience?
- How often do I ask my team members to give me feedback on my leadership style and effectiveness?

Engagement: The heartbeat of a high-performance team

When empowered individuals sense that they are valued members of a winning team, they respond with engagement, the emotional and intellectual commitment a person has towards their role, and towards the broader organization. Engagement goes beyond just job satisfaction. It requires an environment where team members feel part of something meaningful, and believe they are working towards a shared goal. Engagement boosts productivity, fosters innovation, and promotes a positive workplace culture. When individuals operate in an environment of trust, they feel free to grow and develop, and their sense of engagement is further strengthened when they feel that their contributions are appreciated and valued.

> In an engaged team, members show up emotionally and intellectually, not just physically, and are willing to go above and beyond.

In an engaged team, members show up emotionally and intellectually, not just physically, and are willing to go above and beyond.

A leader's role in fostering engagement is critical because engagement represents more than just "doing a job". It is about becoming immersed in the mission and culture of both the team and the organization, and it reflects the profound satisfaction that comes from being part of a collective endeavor and contributing towards its success.

In *Drive: The Surprising Truth About What Motivates Us*, author Daniel Pink points out that humans are primarily motivated by autonomy, mastery, and purpose, factors that go beyond traditional notions of reward and recognition, and tap into the concept of engagement.

- **Autonomy** relates to having control over one's work. It is about the freedom to decide when to work, how to work, what to work on, and who to work with. In a high-performance team, granting autonomy signifies trust in team members' abilities, and acknowledges their capacity to make important decisions.
- **Mastery** is the desire to become proficient at something that matters. It's about improving skills and knowledge. Leaders can promote mastery by setting challenging tasks and providing opportunities for learning and growth. When team members feel that their expertise and skills are valued, their level of engagement increases.
- **Purpose** is the yearning to do things that have meaning and importance, and believing that the work we do has value. A clear, compelling purpose makes each team member feel that they are part of a winning team, working towards a meaningful goal.

As a leader, you can facilitate engagement by creating an environment that invites participation, grants autonomy, promotes mastery, and fosters a sense of purpose. Engaged and motivated individuals are more likely to remain with the organization, and put in the extra effort required to deliver a superior performance.

SPARKLE: A model for effective team engagement

SPARKLE, my model for improving engagement within teams, is synonymous with a seven-pointed star, where each point represents one element of team dynamics. Rooted in neuroscience, it incorporates a tool for assessing current levels of engagement. By adopting the seven elements, leaders can build a high-performance team that is resilient, motivated, and deeply connected to each other and their shared objectives.

1. **Shared vision** The cornerstone of a unified team is a shared vision. Research into the prefrontal cortex by Schacter, Addis, and Buckner reveals its role in visualization and planning.[1] When individuals align with their team's objectives, this region of the brain becomes active,

125

fostering motivation and a sense of belonging. A shared vision is more than just agreeing with common goals; it is envisioning oneself contributing to those goals.

2. **Participation** Active participation transforms team dynamics. When individuals actively engage with the team's objectives, the brain's reward pathways are stimulated. Being involved is about feeling integral to the team. It elevates the experience of teamwork, making it more fulfilling and engaging. These findings are outlined in a study undertaken by Izuma, Saito, and Sadato.[2]

3. **Appreciation** Recognition isn't just good manners; it's a neurochemical trigger. Algoe and Haidt's findings on dopamine, a hormone associated with satisfaction and pleasure, underscore the power of appreciation as an engagement booster.[3] Appreciation not only boosts morale, it also enhances motivation by creating an environment where each success, big or small, is celebrated.

4. **Resilience** The ability to adapt and bounce back is vital in a high-performing team. Resilience ensures that teams not only endure, but can overcome challenges or setbacks, and learn from them. Davidson and McEwen[4] note that resilience is rooted in the brain's neuroplasticity, its innate ability to rewire and adapt.

5. **Knowledge sharing** Sharing our knowledge with others activates the brain's social and communication centers. Promoting a culture of continuous learning ensures that knowledge flows freely. A study by Tamir and Mitchell[5] outlines how the act of sharing knowledge can be personally rewarding, while simultaneously enriching the collective intelligence of the team.

6. **Leadership support** Effective leadership can be a buffer against workplace stress. Individuals who believe they are supported feel more secure and empowered. Supporting your team members, especially when things are not going well, keeps them engaged and productive. Research by Eisenberger[6] points to the impact of support in reducing stress and anxiety.

7. **Empowerment** A measure of autonomy in decision-making plays a significant role in job satisfaction. Empowerment is more than the simple delegation of tasks. It is about entrusting team members with

the freedom to innovate, make decisions, and own their work, which in turn propels engagement and satisfaction. A study by Lee, Reeve, Xue, and Xiong[7] shows that having autonomy to act stimulates motivation and goal-oriented brain regions.

Applying the SPARKLE model

The SPARKLE Team Engagement Analysis and Enhancement Tool will help you determine the current levels of engagement within your team. Once you know this, you can set SMART goals, and create action plans for areas identified as needing improvement. Finally, monitor progress, and make adjustments as necessary.

You can apply the SPARKLE tool as often as needed for continuous assessment, and reassess your strategies to ensure they remain effective. Celebrating milestones will help keep your team engaged and motivated.

Digital tool available at drtomdreyer.com/tools.

SPARKLE Team Engagement, Analysis and Enhancement Tool	
Using the seven SPARKLE elements, assess your team's current levels of engagement. Rate each one on a scale of 1–10 (10 being the highest).	
Current levels of engagement	**Rating (1–10)**
1. Shared vision	
2. Participation	
3. Appreciation	
4. Resilience	
5. Knowledge sharing	
6. Leadership support	
7. Empowerment	

Based on your assessment of the team's levels of engagement, set SMART goals (specific, measurable, attainable, relevant, time-bound) for each element that needs improvement.

SPARKLE element	SMART goals
1. Shared vision	
2. Participation	
3. Appreciation	
4. Resilience	
5. Knowledge sharing	
6. Leadership support	
7. Empowerment	

Once you have set SMART goals, create an action plan for each goal. Include practical steps and deadlines to help your team achieve the desired outcomes.

SMART goals	Action plan	Deadline

Monitor progress made in meeting each SMART goal. Adjust the action plan if necessary, and keep track of progress by updating your ratings.

SMART goals	Start date	Progress tracker	Updated rating	New date

Maslow: A framework for understanding engagement

Developed in 1943 by American psychologist Abraham Maslow, the Hierarchy of Needs is the classic framework to apply to the concept of employee engagement. If engagement is the heartbeat of a high-performance team, then to understand engagement, you need to examine the impulses that underpin it. Maslow's hierarchy has five levels: Survival, Security, Belonging, Self-esteem, and Self-actualization, with each level building on the one before it.

Maslow's Hierarchy of Needs

1. **Survival** This encompasses essential physiological needs, such as food, water, and sleep. If these foundation-level needs are not met, it is almost impossible for any other needs to be met.
2. **Security** Once our basic survival needs are met, we can focus on security and safety, both physical and economic. Stability at home and work is a form of security.
3. **Belonging** Psychologically, our need to belong, and to be loved, finds fulfilment through social interactions with family, friends, colleagues, and community.
4. **Self-esteem** This need is met when we receive recognition and respect from others. Esteem can also take the form of self-respect, self-confidence, and independence.
5. **Self-actualization** This recognizes the need to fulfill our potential, and be the best that we can be. It applies to both our working life and our personal relationships.

Over the decades, many researchers have expanded on the relationship between Maslow's Hierarchy of Needs, and levels of engagement in the workplace. This generates a useful tool to help leaders assess where individual team members stand in their personal lives, as well as in the workplace, and help them move towards a higher level.

Levels of engagement

1. **Disengaged (Survival)** At this level, employees are primarily focused on getting by. They might feel stressed, undervalued, or ignored. They're there for the paycheck and do the minimum required. As a leader, the challenge is to make disengaged team members feel noticed and valued. Recognize their efforts, involve them in decision-making, and emphasize how their work contributes to the team's goals. Giving disengaged individuals the right sort of attention can shift their mindset from Survival to Security.

2. **Not engaged (Security)** Employees may feel secure, but they are not emotionally invested in the team. They do their jobs competently, but don't go beyond their defined roles. The leader's role is to build stronger relationships, foster a sense of belonging, and create opportunities for collaboration and social interactions.

3. **Almost engaged (Belonging)** The first signs of belonging include participating more actively in team activities, and being willing to contribute ideas. As a leader, you can enhance this by recognizing team members' efforts, providing constructive feedback, and offering opportunities for growth and advancement.

4. **Engaged (Self-esteem)** Employees who feel esteemed (important) are genuinely engaged. They take pride in their work, and become more involved in tasks, even going the extra mile to accomplish a goal. To maintain engagement, leaders should acknowledge contributions, provide challenging assignments, and encourage decision-making.

5. **Highly engaged (Self-actualization)** Highly engaged employees are not just invested in their roles, but they are also passionate about the team's mission. They constantly innovate, seek new challenges, and strive to exceed their goals. Leaders can motivate highly engaged employees by fostering an environment that supports continuous learning, promotes creativity, and encourages personal growth.

MATCHING MASLOW'S HIERARCHY OF NEEDS TO LEVELS OF ENGAGEMENT

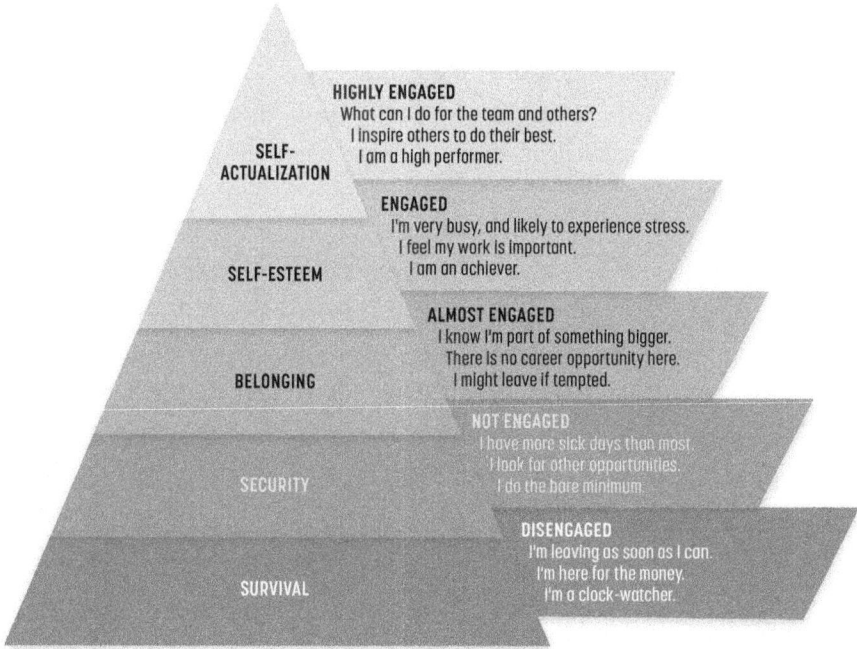

SELF-ACTUALIZATION

HIGHLY ENGAGED
What can I do for the team and others?
I inspire others to do their best.
I am a high performer.

SELF-ESTEEM

ENGAGED
I'm very busy, and likely to experience stress.
I feel my work is important.
I am an achiever.

BELONGING

ALMOST ENGAGED
I know I'm part of something bigger.
There is no career opportunity here.
I might leave if tempted.

SECURITY

NOT ENGAGED
I have more sick days than most.
I look for other opportunities.
I do the bare minimum.

SURVIVAL

DISENGAGED
I'm leaving as soon as I can.
I'm here for the money.
I'm a clock-watcher.

GRPI: A model for team effectiveness

Maslow's Hierarchy of Needs can be applied in the context of engagement, but now let's turn to effectiveness. The GRPI model was developed by organizational theorist Richard Beckhard in 1972, as a framework for enhancing effectiveness in high-performance teams. It comprises four elements: Goals, Roles and Responsibilities, Processes and Procedures, and Interpersonal Relationships (or Interactions).

1. **Goals** The first step is to establish what the team needs to achieve. Goals should be specific, measurable, achievable, relevant, and time-bound (SMART). All members of high-performance teams should share a clear understanding of their goals, with everyone knowing not only what the end goal is, but why it matters, and what performance

standards are expected of them. As a leader, you need to ensure that the goals are communicated to all team members. Goals can evolve over time, so be prepared to recalibrate and realign as necessary.

2. **Roles and responsibilities** Each team member should have a well-defined role, and understand how all the roles fit together. This includes knowing what needs to be done, who is responsible for doing what, and the order in which to do things. Clarifying assigned responsibilities and expected performance standards will ensure that all team members understand how their own work contributes to the overall goal. Clarity helps prevent confusion, overlap, or gaps in responsibilities.

3. **Processes and procedures** These set out how a team communicates, coordinates, and collaborates. Having effective processes in place allows a team to work together to complete tasks efficiently. This might include project planning, setting milestones, tracking progress, resolving conflicts, and decision-making. As a leader, you must ensure that your team has access to the resources they need, and that any obstacles to achieving their goals are removed.

4. **Interpersonal relationships** The way team members interact with each other, both professionally and personally, can significantly impact team performance. Good interpersonal relationships encompass open communication, trust, respect, and inclusion.

GRPI MODEL OF TEAM EFFECTIVENESS

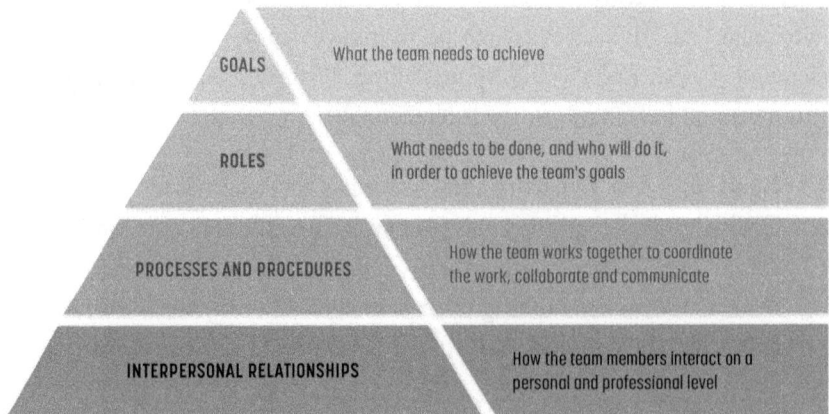

GOALS	What the team needs to achieve
ROLES	What needs to be done, and who will do it, in order to achieve the team's goals
PROCESSES AND PROCEDURES	How the team works together to coordinate the work, collaborate and communicate
INTERPERSONAL RELATIONSHIPS	How the team members interact on a personal and professional level

Belbin Team Inventory: Maximizing team dynamics

The Belbin Team Inventory (BTI) puts forward the notion that effective teams usually comprise a diverse mix of individuals, each fulfilling a different role, based on their strengths and/or preferences. Dr Raymond Meredith Belbin identified nine roles that contribute to a team's success. By understanding these roles (or clusters of behaviorable attributes), leaders can assimilate their team's unique dynamic to maximize performance and manage potential weaknesses. The BTI is a practical tool that helps leaders form balanced teams and develop skills. Remember, the goal isn't to pigeonhole individuals into specific roles, but to appreciate the diversity of skills and perspectives within a team.

Belbin's nine roles for team success

1. **Plant** – Innovators and idea generators who thrive on creativity, and frequently offer new concepts and unconventional solutions.
   - **Strengths** Imaginative and free-thinking. They generate ideas and solve difficult problems.
   - **Weaknesses** Can be preoccupied with their own thoughts, leading them to overlook others' perspectives. May ignore practical details, and can be overly optimistic about their ideas.
   - **Leadership actions** Maximize their creativity by allocating tasks that will encourage them to translate their ideas into practical solutions or applications.

2. **Resource Investigator** – Explorers who are naturally curious, outgoing and enthusiastic. They are always on the lookout for new developments and opportunities.
   - **Strengths** Good communicators who are not afraid to tackle new things. Good at making and developing contacts.
   - **Weaknesses** Can be overly optimistic; may lose interest once initial enthusiasm has passed.

133

- **Leadership actions** Utilize their networking skills. Encourage them to establish relationships with other team members, and stick with tasks until completion.

3. **Coordinator** – Natural team leaders who excel at delegating, setting goals, and encouraging others to work towards these goals.
   - **Strengths** Mature and confident, they identify talent and delegate tasks effectively.
   - **Weaknesses** Can be seen as manipulative. May be eager to offload their share of work.
   - **Leadership actions** Encourage them to be more hands-on and ensure their delegation is seen as fair and balanced.

4. **Shaper** – The drivers of the team, they challenge others to improve and perform better. They are dynamic, with a high level of motivation and a desire to achieve.
   - **Strengths** Thrive on pressure, and have the persistence to overcome obstacles.
   - **Weaknesses** Can be argumentative and may sometimes offend people's feelings.
   - **Leadership actions** Value their drive, but encourage them to be more empathic and respectful in their dealings with others.

5. **Monitor/Evaluator** – They excel at monitoring and evaluating situations. Capable of making impartial judgments, and applying logical reasoning, they consider all options before making decisions.
   - **Strengths** Serious, strategic, and discerning.
   - **Weaknesses** Can be overly critical, and may not be able to inspire others. May lack personal drive.
   - **Leadership actions** Encourage them to communicate their suggestions in a constructive and inspiring manner.

6. **Team worker** – The peacemakers of the team, they willingly provide support, and ensure that everyone works together effectively.
   - **Strengths** Cooperative, perceptive, and diplomatic. They listen, and avert friction.
   - **Weaknesses** Can be indecisive in crunch situations and tend to avoid confrontation.
   - **Leadership actions** Recognize their contribution to team morale. Encourage them to be more decisive.

7. **Implementer** – They get things done, and can turn ideas and concepts into practical actions and workable plans.
   - **Strengths** Practical, reliable, efficient, and good organizers.
   - **Weaknesses** May be inflexible and resistant to change.
   - **Leadership actions** Appreciate their practicality, but encourage them to be open to new ideas.

8. **Completer/Finisher** – Detail-oriented, and always on the lookout for errors and omissions. They make sure that every task is completed thoroughly.
   - **Strengths** Painstaking and conscientious, but sometimes anxious. They search out errors, polish and perfect.
   - **Weaknesses** Can be prone to worry, and are often reluctant to delegate.
   - **Leadership actions** Reassure them of their team's trust. Encourage them to delegate tasks when necessary.

9. **Specialist** – Technical experts who contribute essential skills, knowledge, and expertise.
   - **Strengths** Single-minded, self-starting, and dedicated.
   - **Weaknesses** May dwell on details. May not contribute much outside their field of expertise.
   - **Leadership actions** Encourage them to consider the big picture and communicate their knowledge, so other team members can learn from them.

BELBIN'S NINE TEAM ROLES

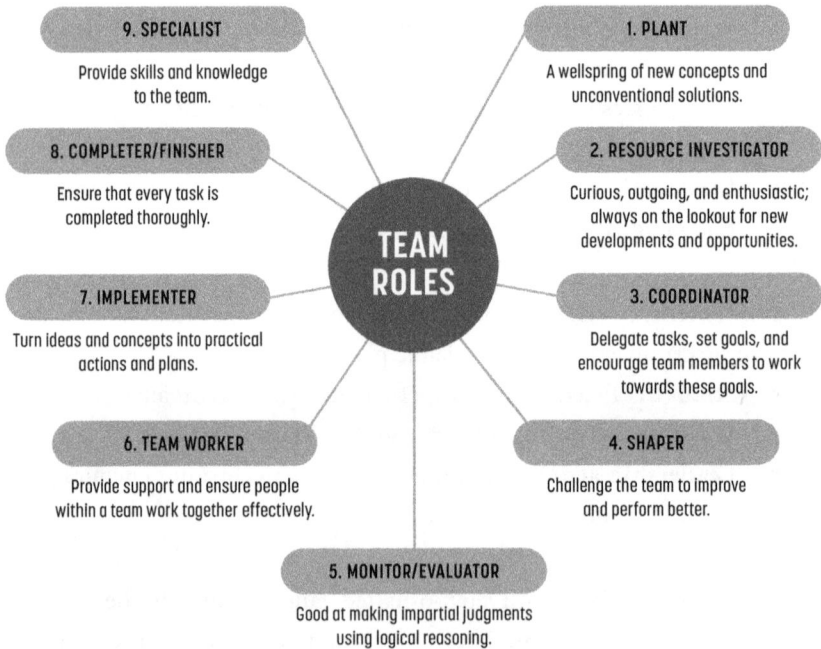

9. SPECIALIST
Provide skills and knowledge to the team.

8. COMPLETER/FINISHER
Ensure that every task is completed thoroughly.

7. IMPLEMENTER
Turn ideas and concepts into practical actions and plans.

6. TEAM WORKER
Provide support and ensure people within a team work together effectively.

TEAM ROLES

1. PLANT
A wellspring of new concepts and unconventional solutions.

2. RESOURCE INVESTIGATOR
Curious, outgoing, and enthusiastic; always on the lookout for new developments and opportunities.

3. COORDINATOR
Delegate tasks, set goals, and encourage team members to work towards these goals.

4. SHAPER
Challenge the team to improve and perform better.

5. MONITOR/EVALUATOR
Good at making impartial judgments using logical reasoning.

STORY IN PRACTICE

Creating a cohesive team

City Hospital was renowned for its groundbreaking medical research. One of the research teams was preparing for a study on improving standards of cardiac patient care but, despite their undeniable expertise, they were finding it difficult to work collaboratively. Elena Rodriguez, an external management consultant, was brought in to resolve the problem. Recognizing that the team was made up of high-performing individuals who were accustomed to working independently, she had to find a way to encourage them work together.

She began by setting up a meeting with each team member to talk about their role in the project. Exploring their individual strengths and weaknesses, and levels of engagement, provided insight into which roles or tasks might suit them best.

After considering various models for assessing team performance, she opted for Tuckman's Five Stages of Team Development. Her first step was to outline the goal of the study. Next, she assigned tasks, making sure that everyone understood their roles and responsibilities in the context of the project, as well as the need to work collaboratively to meet the objectives of the study. Informal get-togethers gave team members an opportunity to chat and share insights on the project, and this generated a sense of belonging and common purpose. Elena also built personal trust by listening to individual concerns, and doing her best to address them.

In any team of strong-willed, opinionated individuals, there are inevitably conflicts, but Elena saw these as necessary steps towards reaching a shared understanding. By redefining some roles, and facilitating group discussions to seek common ground, she helped the team through Tuckman's 'storming' phase.

As the conflicts subsided, Elena focused on solidifying team dynamics. With the project starting to meet its milestones, she held open discussions to reflect on what was working, and what required intervention or improvement. Because humility and mutual respect were at the core of her approach, team members accepted constructive criticism without turning it into conflict. She encouraged them to express their views and continued to listen attentively to what they had to say.

When she could see that the team was working well together, Elena focused on keeping the momentum going. She provided regular feedback on the status of the project, made decisions based on consultation and consensus, and celebrated milestones, no matter how small. Her steady guidance kept the team on track, and a shared sense of purpose meant that individual team members willingly accepted the responsibility for meeting their targets.

Ultimately, the team achieved its goal of setting a new standard in cardiac patient care. They were able to do this because Elena understood and harnessed the power of a high-performance team. As the project came to an end, she took time to acknowledge each team member, and thank them for their contributions. She gave constructive feedback to each team member and made sure that everyone was aware of their follow-up tasks, as well as potential future projects.

Elena Rodriguez's story demonstrates how a motivated leader can transform a group of talented individuals into a high-performance team.

SELF-REFLECTION PIT STOP

Scan the QR code or visit drtomdreyer.com/tools to download your e-toolkit.

Assessing high-performance teams

In Golden Star 5, we examined different stages of team development and how teams respond to their intrinsic goals and behaviors. Begin this pit stop by reflecting on the status of your team members. Identify their individual strengths, and note any areas for improvement. Do you consider them to be high-performing? Within the framework of the models described, can you pinpoint any leadership strategies or behaviors that have contributed to your team's performance?

1. **Tuckman's Five Stages of Team Development**
   1. Which of Tuckman's Five Stages (Forming, Storming, Norming, Performing, Adjourning), represents the current state of your team? Knowing this, would you alter or adjust your leadership approach in any way?
   2. Reflect on a time when you successfully led your team through a difficult stage. What strategies did you use?

2. **EACH Mindset Model**
   1. Consider the four pillars (Empowerment, Accountability, Courage, Humility). Reflecting on your leadership style, which pillar is your strongest, and which could use more attention?
   2. How can you incorporate all four pillars into your leadership practice to foster a high-performing team?

3. **SPARKLE: A model for effective team engagement**
   1. Use the SPARKLE model to rate levels of engagement within your team. Can you identify any actions you have taken that have boosted engagement?
   2. If levels of engagement are lower than you would like, what can you do to increase them?

4. Maslow: A framework for understanding engagement

1. If you apply Maslow's Hierarchy of Needs and the corresponding levels of engagement to your leadership style, do you feel that you meet these needs adequately? How can you make better connections with your team?

5. GRPI: A model for team effectiveness

1. Reflect on how your team aligns with the GRPI model. If there are areas that stand out as particularly strong or weak, what could you do to rectify this?

6. Belbin Team Inventory: Maximizing team dynamics

1. Can you identify how many of Belbin's nine team roles are represented within your team, and which roles are missing or underrepresented?
2. Would having a better understanding of these roles enhance your team's performance?

Set SMART goals

Set two or three SMART goals that will enhance your team's overall performance. For example, if you think they could be more cohesive, a goal might be: "Over the next six months, I will implement a monthly team-building activity to improve interaction and levels of engagement." Review these goals regularly to track your progress, and make adjustments to help you stay on track.

Developing a high-performance team is like undertaking a long journey. You need to constantly check that you are on the right road, and change direction if necessary. Golden Star 5 presented six models for assessing team development. Emotional intelligence (EI) lies at the core of each of these models. If a high-performance team is to thrive, the individual members must be capable of understanding their emotions, and managing them in a positive way. We will explore this in Golden Star 6.

Endnotes

1   Schacter, D. L., Addis, D. R., & Buckner, R. L. (2007). Remembering the past to imagine the future: The prospective brain. *Nature Reviews Neuroscience*, 8(9), 657-661.

2   Izuma, K., Saito, D. N., & Sadato, N. (2008). Processing of social and monetary rewards in the human striatum. *Neuron*, 58(2), 284-294.

3   Algoe, S. B., & Haidt, J. (2009). Witnessing excellence in action: The 'other-praising' emotions of elevation, gratitude, and admiration. *The Journal of Positive Psychology*, 4(2), 105-127.

4   Davidson, R. J., & McEwen, B. S. (2012). Social influences on neuroplasticity: Stress and interventions to promote well-being. *Nature Neuroscience*, 15(5), 689-695.

5   Tamir, D. I., & Mitchell, J. P. (2012). Disclosing information about the self is intrinsically rewarding. *Proceedings of the National Academy of Sciences, 109(21)*, 8038-8043.

6   Eisenberger, N. I. (2013). Social ties and health: A social neuroscience perspective on health-related social processes. *Annual Review of Psychology*, 64, 411-433.

7   Lee, W., Reeve, J., Xue, Y., & Xiong, J. (2012). Neural differences between intrinsic reasons for doing versus extrinsic reasons for doing: An fMRI study. *Neuroscience Research*, 73(1), 68-72.

GOLDEN STAR

6

THE POWER OF EI AND NLP

Emotional intelligence (EI) is the ability to identify, understand, and manage emotions. It is the capacity to be aware of, control, and express our own emotions, and handle interpersonal relationships judiciously and empathically. It is a powerful force that, when used properly, will enhance your leadership capacity in ways that are both tangible and emotionally resonant. Emotional intelligence is not only transformative, it is also deeply human-centered.

> Emotional intelligence is a powerful force that will enhance your leadership capacity.

This Golden Star examines the profound impact of emotional intelligence, which forms the bedrock of most relationships. You will learn how to nurture EI in yourself and others, and how to harness the power of your mind through neurolinguistic programming (NLP). By applying these insights, you can become a leader who not only inspires your team, but connects with them on a deeper level.

Motivational coach, Tony Robbins, says, "The quality of your life is the quality of your relationships." We could modify this to, "The quality of your leadership is the quality of your relationships with your team."

Similarly, self-improvement guru, Dale Carnegie says, "You can make more friends in two months by becoming interested in people than you can in two years by trying to get people interested in you."

Leading with emotional intelligence

The concept of emotional intelligence was first identified by Peter Salovey and John D. Mayer in the 1960s, and popularized by psychologist and author Daniel Goleman in his 1995 book, *Emotional Intelligence: Why it can matter more than IQ.*

Neuroscientifically, stress triggers the amygdala, a part of the brain involved in emotional responses. When we are stressed, we don't always think clearly or act rationally. Leaders who can manage their emotional response to stress tend to remain composed under pressure. These leaders are usually capable of turning challenges into opportunities for growth, learning and personal development.

Emotionally intelligent leaders are authentic and ethical. They are mindful of the impact of their decisions, and strive to promote fairness, transparency, and respect. They champion positivity, and encourage collaborative problem-solving. In a team environment, the result is a culture of trust, where team members feel comfortable expressing their emotions and ideas without fear of judgment.

> Neuroscience shows that emotions can be contagious, which means that a team with high EI can positively influence the culture or mindset of other teams in an organization.

Leaders can foster emotional intelligence within a team by creating an environment of trust. Neuroscience shows that emotions can be contagious, which means that a team with high EI can positively influence the culture or mindset of other teams in an organization. By anticipating and navigating any emotional undercurrents, emotionally intelligent leaders can transform their team into a cohesive unit, where individuals operate with a degree of autonomy, but at the same time are aware of, and respond to, the emotional cues of other team members.

Sustaining emotional intelligence involves sustaining a culture of personal development and growth. Leaders and team members need to reinforce EI behaviors in order to set certain patterns within their neural networks. These behaviors include embracing mindfulness, consciously regulating your emotions, listening with empathy, and seeking feedback.

In the future, emotional intelligence is likely to play an increasing role in leadership. As workplaces become more diverse and dynamic, the ability to connect with team members on an emotional level will be essential.

What is empathy?

In its simplest form, empathy is the ability to understand and share another person's feelings; their joy, pain, fears and hopes. We often encounter empathy as a heart-tugging, tear-jerking sentiment in romantic novels or movies, but empathy is not found just in print or on screen. It is a tangible and transformative emotion that every effective leader should master.

Cultivating empathy requires comprehension, compassion, and interpersonal connection. But you might ask, "What's in it for me?" Besides the benefits of understanding your team better, increased empathy has a ripple effect that can benefit any organization.

In a leadership context, empathy means responding to others with kindness, and acting in a way that supports them. This builds an environment of trust and loyalty, facilitates conflict resolution, and fosters a deeper connection with your team. The result is improved morale, increased engagement, and enhanced productivity.

Empathy also provides a psychological "safety net", a space where your team members are not afraid to voice ideas, take risks, or express their feelings. In this way, empathy promotes creativity and innovation, and we all know how much business today thrives on innovation!

> When you strive to understand the feelings and perspectives of others, you will make choices that are not just beneficial to your organization, but also considerate of the individuals involved.

However, before you set out to understand others, it's essential to develop self-empathy. Acknowledge your own emotions, recognize your needs, and respond with self-compassion. Empathy for oneself creates a foundation upon which you can develop empathy for others.

Empathy acts as a moral compass, guiding you towards ethical decisions. When you strive to understand the feelings and perspectives of others, you will make choices that are not just beneficial to your organization, but also considerate of the individuals involved.

But what if you don't think you have empathy? Well, it can be developed. Through a blend of active listening, keen observation, openness, and a genuine interest in people, you can cultivate empathy. And like any muscle, the more you exercise it, the stronger it gets.

Of course, empathy has its challenges. Being constantly aware of other peoples' emotions can lead to compassion fatigue. You need to set boundaries that will prevent you from becoming too caught up in your teams' personal issues, and becoming emotionally drained. Remember, empathy is not about solving everyone's problems; it is about understanding them.

Harnessing the power of NLP in leadership

Neurolinguistic programming (NLP) is a technique designed to alter established patterns of thought and behavior, and raise self-awareness. The concept first appeared in 1975, in the *The Structure of Magic* by Richard Bandler and John Grinder, who developed an approach to communication and personal development that would help people reshape their thoughts and behavior patterns to achieve desired outcomes.

You've probably heard the phrase "it's all in the mind". What if I told you that, as a leader, you could harness the power of not just your own mind, but also the minds of your team members, to optimize performance, improve communication, and inspire greatness? Intrigued?

Welcome to neurolinguistic programming. NLP is based on four key elements: sensory acuity, representational systems, submodalities, and anchoring. Let's examine them.

Sensory acuity

Sensory acuity is the ability to read and interpret silent cues given by others. In a busy work environment, these almost-imperceptible signals often go unnoticed, but leaders who can correctly interpret them have access to a powerful tool.

Picture yourself presiding over a meeting. As you present an innovative idea, a shadow of doubt momentarily clouds a colleague's eyes, or a slight twitch of the lips betrays an unspoken concern. With sensory acuity, these fleeting signals reveal underlying emotions or beliefs. Intuitive observation enables you to observe other people's emotions and reactions, allowing you to adjust your communication strategy in real time. But can one develop sensory acuity? Absolutely, and here's how:

> Sensory acuity is the ability to read and interpret silent cues given by others.

- **Embrace mindful observation** Contrary to what many believe, observing is an active task. The next time you are with your team, don't be just physically present. Instead, immerse yourself in the moment. Focus on each individual's responses, both verbal and non-verbal, and try to perceive the emotions driving these responses. Mindful observation is the first step.

- **Listen carefully** The way we say things, known as vocal tonality, often reveals more than our words alone. For example, is someone's voice hesitant, even though they're speaking words of affirmation? Or is it laced with an enthusiasm that their words don't convey? By tuning into tonal shifts, you'll glean insights into genuine sentiments, or potential reservations.

- **Study body language** Body language provides non-verbal cues. A sudden crossing of arms might signify defensiveness, while constant finger-tapping could be a sign of impatience, or anxiety. When a team member unconsciously mimics your posture (known as mirroring), it could indicate agreement or rapport.

- **Observe energy levels** Although energy levels are not always easily observed, they can indicate a person's state of mind. Just as a barometer rises or falls in response to changes in air pressure, energy levels are affected by things like workplace stress, disagreement with the topic at hand, or sheer disinterest. By noticing subtle shifts, you may be able to address a team member's concerns even before they've been voiced.

- **Reflect and adjust** At the end of every period of interaction with others, such as a meeting or training session, take a moment to reflect. If you observed unexpected reactions, ask yourself if you might have missed any cues. Over time, these reflective exercises will allow you to refine your observational skills, until they become second nature.

Sensory acuity allows you to establish genuine connections through authentic, empathic communication. As you acquire this skill, remember that watching people is not about prying or spying, but about seeking to understand, and fostering transparency and trust.

Representational systems: How we learn

We process information via neural pathways in the brain, which steer information into diverse patterns, allowing us to absorb new things. NLP calls these pathways "representational systems." Just as a city planner must understand every part of a road network to optimize traffic flow, a leader should be adept at leveraging the power of representational systems for maximum team efficiency. Identifying individual preferences, and adopting a flexible approach to communications will improve clarity and comprehension. You will also be validating each team member's unique learning style. A communication strategy that speaks to all members of your team will foster an environment of inclusivity and respect.

Representational systems are symptomatic of how we learn. They trace back to our formative sensory experiences of sight, sound and touch. Remember the enjoyment you got from your first picture books, the rhythm of a spoken nursery rhyme, or using finger paints? Let's look at how our earliest impulses continue to influence our learning patterns:

- **Visual learners** These individuals thrive on imagery, and need to see things in order to understand them. They use words to paint a picture, and their thought processes often mirror a dynamic storyboard, populated with vivid imagery, charts, and diagrams.

    When addressing visual learners, choose compelling visuals, such as PowerPoint slides, infographics, and flowcharts. Use descriptive language to create mental images. Phrases like "imagine this scenario" or "picture this" are particularly effective.

- **Auditory learners** They respond to the sound of words, to resonance, rhythm, and tone. They prefer oral explanations, they can easily recall conversations, and they may subconsciously repeat things aloud to help them retain the information.

    Capture their attention through dialogue, discussion, and brainstorming sessions, and make use of voice notes and podcasts. Encourage them to voice their thoughts. Tone of voice is crucial, so varying your tone for emphasis can help drive a point home.

149

- **Kinesthetic learners** These tactile, hands-on learners are all about touch and feel. Because they need to experience something to understand it, abstract concepts can seem alien until they've felt them through practical application or experience.

   They learn best when they're actively involved, so offer workshops, on-the-job training, and role-playing exercises. Use props to help explain new ideas, and encourage walking meetings, since movement can stimulate thought processes.

Decoding submodalities: Fine-tuning our sensory perceptions

In NLP, sensory experiences are referred to as submodalities. Think of them as the brightness, contrast, and saturation settings on your television. Just as subtle adjustments can enhance or dampen the viewing experience, fine-tuning our submodalities can recalibrate our emotional responses. In life, our perception of reality comprises not just what we see or hear, but how we interpret events through our senses.

As individuals, our submodalities are shaped by our experiences and interpretations. Tapping into sensory perceptions allows leaders to motivate, guide, influence, and respond to team members in ways that resonate on a profoundly personal level. To decode individual submodalities, leaders need to engage in active listening and passive observation.

- **Visual submodalities**
   Visual experiences aren't just about *what* we see, but *how* we see. Brightness, distance, size, or even the frame (as in a movie or still image) can impact the emotions tied to a visual memory. The key to decoding this submodality is to try to see what the other person is seeing.

   If a team member experiences self-doubt, or fears tackling a new task, ask them to visualize past successes. Encourage them to amplify positive sensations by making the image bigger or brighter, or by turning a static memory into a dynamic, victorious movie reel. This can enhance confidence and motivation.

- **Auditory submodalities**

  Speech isn't merely sound; it comprises tone, volume, tempo, and direction. The same words whispered softly, or shouted loudly, can convey vastly different emotions.

  During feedback sessions, be conscious of your tone and volume. Constructive criticism may be better received if given in a calm, steady manner. On the other hand, an upbeat tempo is appropriate for cheering on your team.

- **Kinesthetic submodalities**

  Physical sensations can embody emotions. For example, a warm embrace might evoke feelings of comfort or security, while a cold, distant greeting could trigger feelings of loneliness or rejection.

  To foster team bonding, share memories of positive achievements and how they made you feel. If discussing challenges, frame them as easily surmountable obstacles rather than burdens to be overcome.

- **Olfactory and gustatory submodalities**

  Although less commonly addressed in a professional context, our senses of smell and taste are powerful memory triggers. For example, a particular aroma can instantly transport us back to a specific time or place.

  Create memorable team meetings by incorporating scents or flavors. Something as simple as the aroma of a special blend of coffee, or freshly baked cookies, can have a positive impact.

Anchoring: Emotional alchemy

"Anchoring" is an emotional remote control, a means to consciously associate certain stimuli with specific emotions. Our brain loves patterns. Whenever it recognizes a consistent pairing between a trigger (such as a song) and an emotional response (remembering a first love), it creates a neural link. Over time, just the trigger alone stimulates the response. Anchoring is like having a curated playlist where every track evokes a distinct emotion. In a team setting, leaders have the power to cue tracks at exactly the right moment to generate harmony, motivation, and a desire for excellence.

To set up anchors for your team, remind them of a successful milestone they have achieved. Ask them to recall how they felt. Next, select a stimulus that captures the moment. Over time, this will serve as an anchor to revive those positive feelings.

- **Choose the emotional state** Start by clearly defining the desired emotional state you want to evoke. It could be confidence, pride, enthusiasm, or any other positive emotion.
- **Identify the stimulus** This could be a specific sound (like tapping a table), a word or phrase ("power on!"), a gesture (thumbs-up), or a song. The key is consistency.
- **Elicit the state** Recall an occasion when the team collectively experienced the desired emotion. At the peak of this recollection, introduce the chosen stimulus. Repeat this process several times to solidify the link.
- **Utilize anchors effectively** Before embarking on a challenging project, encourage the team to choose a dedicated anchor. When morale dips, the anchor can offer a much-needed boost by reconnecting everyone with their initial enthusiasm.
- **Create shared anchors** These could be anything from chanting a motivational phrase at the start of meetings to a celebratory ritual at the conclusion of a successful project, or a unique salutation on team emails. Shared anchors help foster unity.
- **Observe habits and behavior** Individuals may have their own anchors, like wearing a particular item of clothing for presentations, or always choosing the same seat in the room. Recognizing personal anchors will help you reinforce positive behaviors.
- **Avoid negative anchors** Avoid doing things like always giving negative feedback in the same venue, as this can lead to anxiety every time the team gathers in that space.

Anchors are not only useful for teams. As a leader, you can establish any number of personal anchors, depending on your needs. Then, for example, you can tap into your motivation anchor on days when you feel sluggish, or activate your confidence anchor before a challenging meeting.

Applying NLP techniques

Here are four ways in which you can apply NLP techniques and tools to your leadership style.

1. **Self-awareness** A leader's job is to manage others. But what about managing ourselves? NLP techniques for mastering your inner world include self-awareness (self-reflection), setting goals, and focusing on successful outcomes. Self-awareness means observing our thoughts, emotions, and behaviors without judgment. This allows us to identify any limiting beliefs, and transform them into empowering ones. Set SMART goals and work towards them. To boost motivation and increase your chances of achieving these goals, apply NLP techniques, such as visualization and positive affirmations.

2. **Effective communication** Your words matter. Communication is not just about what you say, but how you say it. When we communicate, even silence speaks volumes. NLP tools for effective communication include building rapport, calibration and language patterns. Building rapport is about establishing connections with others. It's as simple as mirroring someone's body language, matching their verbal tone and pace, or finding common ground. Calibration involves interpreting non-verbal cues or "unspoken words", and responding accordingly. Language patterns, or framing, is the use of key words to influence thoughts, emotions and actions.

3. **Influencing and inspiring** Influential leaders inspire others to achieve a shared vision. NLP techniques include adopting metaphors and storytelling to inspire and motivate, and using language patterns (framing) to persuade and influence. But remember to always act with integrity. While NLP gives you the tools to influence people, it's crucial to use these tools ethically and respectfully.

4. **Enhancing emotional intelligence** If emotional intelligence (EI) is a leader's secret weapon, NLP is a game-changer! It enables leaders to understand themselves and their team members on a deeper level, communicate more effectively, and inspire action. NLP teaches us how to manage our emotions, develop empathy, and improve our interpersonal skills. By employing submodalities, we can alter our emotional responses, such as moving from anger to calmness, or reducing anxiety levels.

NLP is a powerful, practical tool that can enhance leadership skills at all levels, but mastering it takes time and practice. Be patient with yourself, learn continually, and stay committed to the process. As the saying goes, "the view is worth the climb".

Let's look at three leaders who exemplify how the power of NLP can be harnessed to make a positive impact on our society:

Steve Jobs, the legendary co-founder of Apple, was renowned for his captivating presentations and speeches. His secret? Jobs used metaphors and storytelling to inspire his audience, and anchoring techniques to elicit specific emotional responses.

Barack Obama, 44th President of the USA, used NLP techniques in his speeches. By adjusting his tone, pace, and volume, and using persuasive language patterns, Obama was able to inspire millions.

Oprah Winfrey, media mogul and philanthropist, is renowned for her empathic interviewing style. Empathy, a key component of emotional intelligence, is cultivated through NLP techniques.

STORY IN PRACTICE

Unlocking the power of NLP

Edward Patel, founder of EP Finance, had a vision for the future, but his company was not living up to his vision. Edward believed he was doing everything "right". He was implementing a long-term strategy, setting clear goals, and communicating effectively, yet something was missing...

Edward had developed an app that generated financial instruments for maximizing long-term wealth. When he launched his start-up with a few close collaborators, their mission was to transform personal finance for young, affluent professionals. As they expanded, the start-up grew into a conventional mid-sized firm. Edward was determined his company would become a dominant player in the field of online finance, but not everyone shared his zeal. For some employees, working at EP Finance was "just a job", a phrase Edward hated.

After Edward attended a seminar on EI and NLP, he wondered whether NLP could help transform his company. Accepting that transformation begins with self-awareness, he decided to become more emotionally intelligent and empathic. He began with personal mindfulness, paying close attention to his thoughts, feelings, and reactions. He soon recognized a tendency to let stress overshadow his interactions, resulting in abrupt communications, and hasty decision-making. With this newfound aware-ness, Edward sought to manage his emotions better. NLP techniques taught him to reframe stressful situations into opportunities instead of obstacles, while visualizing positive outcomes helped him approach challenges with calmness and clarity.

Edward introduced NLP to his team leaders in a group session. He asked them to use techniques such as sensory acuity, representational systems, and submodalities to uncover any underlying causes for disengagement or dissatisfaction among their team members. He also suggested that they find a way to generate excitement for their team's product or function.

As he was speaking, Edward applied his own sensory acuity to discern any reticence or reluctance among his leaders. Samantha Norris seemed particularly skeptical. She said nothing overtly, and nodded affirmatively as Edward talked, but kept her arms crossed, and appeared disengaged, frequently glancing out of the window. Edward noticed that she struggled to stay focused on the presentation slides.

A few days after the group session, Edward met one-on-one with each leader to gauge their understanding of, and belief in, NLP. In his meeting with Sam, his goal was to uncover her concerns. Suspecting that she was an auditory learner, he knew words would be the best way to convince her of the merits of NLP. At first, she said all the right things, but Edward would have none of that. "We've known each other for a long time, Sam, so tell me the truth. Do you think there are different types of learners?" Edward felt that

NLP's representational systems were something Sam might support. She expressed general agreement, but said that not all new information could be conveyed purely in one of the modes (visual, auditory, and kinesthetic). Edward agreed, but pointed out that key communications could incorporate aspects of each. This opened the way for future discussions.

Over time, Edward and Sam discussed everything from sensory acuity and representational systems to submodalities. In one conversation, he asked Sam to think about the tone she used in meetings, and whether a calm, supportive tone might work better than the strident tone she adopted to motivate her team. Their final meeting concerned anchoring; the technique Sam was most wary about. "Sam," said Edward, "Just try it for yourself. For relaxation, which we can all use." Pointing to a photograph of a yacht on her desk, he asked, "Is that your boat?". When Sam nodded, Edward continued: "Whenever you're tense, think about being on the water. Feel the breeze, and let your imagination drift until a sensation of calm comes over you."

Gradually, Sam began applying NLP techniques herself. They helped her gain insights into her team members' aspirations, fears, and struggles, and she became more tolerant. Establishing her meetings as a safe space, she encouraged open conversations where everyone felt heard. The next time Edward sat in on a meeting, he couldn't believe his ears. As the meeting adjourned, the rousing opening of "Eye of the Tiger" began playing. Sam explained that the song, chosen by vote, was the anchor for the fighting spirit she wanted to instill in every team member. With "Eye of the Tiger" echoing in his head as he returned to his office, Edward decided that his twice-yearly staff meetings should also conclude with a rousing song. But which one should he choose?

As other team leaders adopted NLP and expanded their knowledge of anchoring, rapport-building, and language patterns, they began to communicate more persuasively and influence their teams positively. They used storytelling to inspire their teams, and aligned their objectives with the company's goal of becoming an authority in online finance. In conversations, meetings and presentations, the leaders' compelling message resonated with every member of their team.

Once team members began to feel valued and respected, collaboration between teams improved, resulting in an overall boost in performance. Products were enhanced, and customer satisfaction soared. Within a year, EP Finance was well on its way to achieving its goal.

Edward Patel's story is a testament to the transformative power of emotional intelligence, empathy, and NLP. While NLP provided the techniques for renewed enthusiasm and motivation, it was Edward's embracing of EI and empathy that enabled him to convince even his most skeptical leaders to try the NLP approach. Edward evolved from being a leader who merely directed, to one who connected, inspired, and motivated. The way he transformed his company shows us that the emotional and empathic aspects of leadership are not just "nice-to-haves"; they are essential for success.

SELF-REFLECTION PIT STOP

Scan the QR code or visit drtomdreyer.com/tools to download your e-toolkit.

EI, empathy and NLP

1. Personal EI audit

1. Reflect on your personal level of emotional intelligence (EI), taking cognizance of factors such as self-awareness, motivation, and empathy.
2. Identify areas where you can improve, and set goals to enhance your emotional intelligence in those areas.

2. Empathy in action

1. Recall a recent situation where you demonstrated empathy. What was the outcome?
2. Can you think of a situation where showing more empathy might have resulted in a better outcome? What can you do to harness the power of empathy in future interactions?

3. Foster a culture of EI and empathy

1. Does your team display emotional intelligence and empathy? If not, what can you do to change this?
2. Set SMART goals to cultivate such a culture.

4. Manage emotions

1. Leadership requires you to handle stress and manage emotions. Reflect on how you manage your own emotional challenges, as well as those experienced by your team. What strategies work for you, and what strategies could you improve?
2. Set goals to improve your emotional resilience.

5. Apply NLP techniques

1. Which NLP techniques discussed in this Golden Star could you apply in your own leadership practice?
2. Choose two techniques, and draft an action plan detailing how you will apply them in the next month.

6. Learning and growth

1. Leadership development is a continuous journey. What lessons will you take away from Golden Star 6, and how will you implement them in your leadership practice?
2. Write down three things you have learned, along with how you plan to apply them.

7. Set SMART goals

Based on all your reflections, set 2–3 SMART goals to improve your team's performance. For example, to increase your team's EI, you might say: "I will take one step in each of the next three months to strengthen my team's sense of emotional safety."

Review your reflections and goals regularly and adjust them as necessary. Leading a high-performance team requires effort, but leadership is not about being perfect; it is about making a commitment to grow, and taking consistent action to accomplish that. Regular reflection will enable you to lead with emotional intelligence, utilize the power of NLP, and practice empathy and understanding in your dealings with others. Remember that emotions are not restricted to our personal lives; they are also part of our organizational culture.

Neurolinguistic programming enables us to calibrate our communication, build rapport, and influence more effectively. But, like any leadership tool, its efficacy depends on how skillfully it is used. Emotional intelligence and empathy ensure that NLP techniques are employed in an ethical, people-centered manner.

In the next Golden Star, we'll look at different forms of communication and discover some tools and techniques that will help you master this vital leadership skill.

GOLDEN STAR

7

MASTERING COMMUNICATION

Effective communication is about listening with purpose, and speaking with clarity and conviction. This Golden Star explores core communication skills, including effective listening, and non-verbal communication. You'll learn how to adapt your messaging style to the audience, give feedback and constructive criticism, and ask impactful questions. We'll also touch briefly on presentation skills, and storytelling.

> Leaders who excel in communication operate in an environment of clarity, understanding, and mutual respect.

Seeing someone's eyes light up when they grasp the message you are conveying is testament to the power of masterful communication. But if their perplexed expressions suggest a missed message, you will understand the bitterness of miscommunication.

Leaders who excel in communication operate in an environment of clarity, understanding, and mutual respect. When people feel heard and respected, it is easier to influence, inspire, and motivate them.

The art of listening: Going beyond hearing

Two often overlooked aspects of communication are active listening, and non-verbal communication. The best communicators are usually those who know how to *listen*.

Hearing and listening are not the same thing. Hearing is a passive process in which sounds are received by the ear. As one of the five senses (along with sight, sound, taste, and touch), it is purely physiological. Listening, on the other hand, is an active, psychological process that involves the brain's ability to understand and interpret what we sense.

Active (effective) listening is about not just hearing words but grasping the meaning or intention behind them. It occurs when the listener pays attention to the speaker's words, tone, and non-verbal cues, and provides relevant responses or feedback.

Passive listening is when you hear words but don't fully engage with them. This could be due to many factors, including a simple lapse in concentration. We've all had the experience of our mind wandering in the middle of a meeting, or realizing we're thinking about something other than the presentation we are supposed to be listening to.

Changing from a passive listener to an active one requires patience, practice, and persistence, but the rewards include improved understanding, stronger relationships, and enhanced levels of trust.

Neuroscience and the communication process

Neuroscientifically, communication activates various regions of the brain, stimulating neural pathways associated with motivation, trust and collective effort. The prefrontal cortex, which processes higher-order cognitive functions, plays a role in decision-making and social interactions.[1] The limbic system governs emotional responses. The amygdala, a part of the limbic system, regulates emotions and social behavior.[2] Clear, precise communication reduces uncertainty and ambiguity, which our brains naturally resist, and makes us more receptive to changes and new ideas.[3] Working together, these cognitive functions enable us to build and maintain healthy relationships and manage conflict. Authentic communication stimulates the release of oxytocin, which has been shown to enhance our level of trust, and strengthen interpersonal bonds.[4]

Mirror neurons, a type of brain cell that responds when we perform an action and then see someone else repeat the same action, foster empathy and understanding.[5] "Mirroring" the emotional states of others, facilitates empathic responses.

At its most basic, the communication process involves a sender who conveys a message to a receiver. The message could be oral (spoken), non-verbal (written), or conveyed by body language (gesture, posture or facial expressions). How the message is sent and received can be influenced by the emotions, perceptions and/or experiences of both the sender and the receiver.

The sender "encodes" their thoughts or information into a message, which they hope will be understood by the intended receiver. How effectively this is done may depend on the sender's language proficiency, emotional state, perceptions, biases, personal views and/or cultural or social background. Sending a message is not a game of pass the parcel; the intention is not just to deliver a message, but to ensure that the receiver "gets" it.

To this end, the receiver must "decode" the message so that it has meaning for them. This process may be influenced by the receiver's own level of engagement with the topic, their language proficiency, emotional state, perceptions, biases, and/or cultural or social background.

Successful communication occurs when the receiver's decoding matches the sender's encoding. If this is not achieved, the intended message will not be conveyed, or the receiver may not get the whole story, or may misinterpret it.

Feedback closes the communication loop. It is a response from the receiver that lets the sender know how their message was interpreted. Feedback can validate a message, request or provide new information, or trigger a change of approach. It's the echo that returns to you, carrying valuable data about the efficacy of your communication.

Understanding the communication process helps leaders recognize why some messages hit the bullseye, and others miss the mark. It enables you to refine your communication strategies which, in turn, will build stronger connections and facilitate collaboration within your team.

HURIER: A guide to effective listening

The HURIER Listening Profile (HLP) was developed in 1996 by Judi Brownell, author and professor of Organizational Communication. Based on a behavioral approach to listening, it assesses the strengths and weaknesses of a respondent's listening behavior and skills.

- **Hearing** The basic act of hearing the sounds and words spoken by another person.
- **Understanding** Interpreting the meaning of the words and sounds you hear.

- **Remembering** Retaining the information you've understood for future reference.
- **Interpreting** Making sense of the speaker's words and non-verbal cues, and considering their feelings and intentions.
- **Evaluating** Analyzing the message to discern its truth, significance, and relevance.
- **Responding** Providing appropriate feedback to show that you have listened to (heard) and understood the speaker's message.

HURIER MODEL: A GUIDE TO EFFECTIVE LISTENING

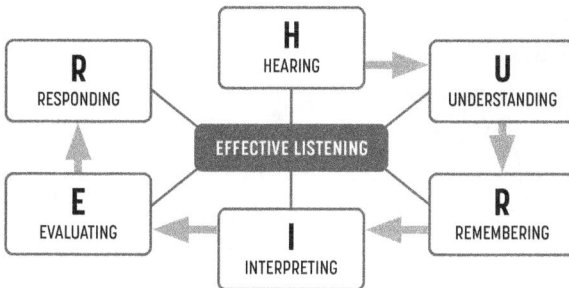

LISTEN: A model for all communications

The LISTEN model, which I designed, enhances both informal and formal communications. It integrates the auditory (hearing) aspects of communication with the visual (seeing), cognitive (thinking), and emotional (feeling) aspects. Speech activates specific areas of the brain: the auditory cortex, which processes sound; the limbic system, which regulates emotions; and the frontal regions, which are responsible for cognitive analysis and empathy. Inspired by the HURIER model, LISTEN can be used in everyday interactions, one-on-one meetings, small group discussions, and formal presentations.

- **Look** Observe non-verbal cues, like facial expressions and body language. These cues can provide insight, and enhance understanding, without interrupting the flow of a conversation.

- **Inquire** Engage with the speaker by asking insightful questions or seeking clarification that deepens the conversation. In a one-on-one or small group setting, you can ask questions directly. To avoid interrupting the speaker in a formal presentation, make notes for a designated Q&A session afterwards.
- **Summarize** Give brief summaries to reinforce understanding. In an informal meeting, you might give direct feedback to the speaker. In group presentations, you could summarize key points to raise during a post-presentation discussion.
- **Tune in** Being emotionally and mentally present is essential in all types of communication, from casual conversations to formal presentations. There will be times when you might have to fend off distractions to remain focused.
- **Empathize** Establishing an empathic connection isn't just a speaker's responsibility. When the listener strives to understand the speaker's emotions and perspectives, it fosters mutual respect, and enhances both hierarchical and peer-to-peer interactions.
- **Nurture** Effective communication is based on mutual trust and respect. To ensure open and honest dialogue, leaders need to cultivate a safe space where everyone feels valued and heard.

THE LISTEN MODEL

L	LOOK	Focus attention on the speaker's non-verbal signals such as body language and facial expressions.
I	INQUIRE	Engage with the speaker by posing insightful questions.
S	SUMMARIZE	Offer periodic summarizations of your understanding.
T	TUNE IN	Maintain a steady emotional and mental presence throughout the conversation.
E	EMPATHIZE	Strive to comprehend the speaker's emotions and viewpoint.
N	NURTURE	Cultivate a safe and respectful atmosphere for communication, enabling open and honest dialogue.

Non-verbal communication: The unspoken language

Non-verbal communication, often referred to as body language, speaks directly to our intrinsic emotions and instincts. A substantial percentage of our day-to-day communications comprises non-verbal communication in the form of facial expressions, posture and gestures, and even silence, all of which can either harmonize with, or clash with, our spoken words. As leaders, observing non-verbal cues gives us insight into the unfiltered feelings and attitudes of our team, allowing us to respond more effectively.

> Faces are emotional billboards, displaying our moods and reactions for everyone to see. A genuine smile can light up a room, whereas a frown casts a shadow of unease.

Mastering non-verbal communication can add depth, nuance, and richness to your interactions. Speaking and listening go beyond what we say or hear. The ancient Greek philosopher, Socrates, said, "Speak, so I may see you." Thousands of years later, his wisdom still applies, particularly to non-verbal communication, which allows us to see beyond the spoken word.

Body language can be a physical manifestation of our inner thoughts and feelings. The way we sit, stand, move, or don't move, all tell a story. Imagine being in a meeting where a team member slouches in his chair, and frequently checks his phone. Without saying a word, he has communicated disinterest and restlessness. Then picture a colleague who leans in, and makes eye contact with everyone. Their non-verbal message is one of confidence and engagement.

Facial expressions are part of body language, but they deserve a special mention. Faces are emotional billboards, displaying our moods and reactions for everyone to see. A genuine smile can light up a room, whereas a frown casts a shadow of unease. Subtle expressions, such as a gentle nod, or raised eyebrow, can signal a range of sentiments, from affirmation to disbelief.

Gestures are the intentional movements and signals we make. They range from demonstrative actions, such as a high-five to celebrate a win, to unconscious movements, such as fidgeting with our spectacles or clothing when we're nervous.

Understanding and using non-verbal cues

To improve your understanding and use of non-verbal communication, and enhance rapport with your team, see how many of these cues you can adopt in your day-to-day interactions.

- **Observe** Pay attention to the visual cues provided by body language. In meetings, are people sitting upright or slouching; are their gestures relaxed or tense; do their facial expressions align with what they are saying or hearing?
- **Contextualize** Consider the circumstances. The purpose or tone of a meeting can alter the meaning of a non-verbal communication. For example, a clenched fist could indicate anger, determination, or triumph, depending on the situation.
- **Be consistent** Look for consistency between verbal and non-verbal communications. Does someone nod or smile when they agree with something, or maintain a neutral expression? Incongruity might point to hidden feelings or unspoken issues.
- **Cultural awareness** Be aware of cultural differences that might impact on non-verbal communication. A gesture that is considered polite in one culture might be offensive in another. For example, in some cultures, a woman may be hesitant to make eye contact when talking to an unfamiliar man.
- **Mirroring** Subtly mirroring another person's body language can create a sense of camaraderie and understanding. However, it is crucial that this comes across as natural and not mimicking.
- **Positive reinforcement** Use appropriate non-verbal cues to reinforce your words, such as nodding when you agree with a point, or smiling when you acknowledge someone.
- **Open posture** Adopting an open posture in meetings or one-on-one conversations suggests an inviting and inclusive atmosphere. However, it is important to be sensitive to cultural, gender, and situational contexts. For example, while crossing your arms in a meeting might be construed as defensive, it can sometimes be necessary to maintain personal space;

just think about an economy flight! In societies where physical contact between genders is restricted, both men and women may adopt "closed" postures to minimize contact. The goal is to remain approachable and engaged, while bearing in mind that an individual's posture may have as much to do with the situation as it does with the message.

Verbal communication: Speaking with clarity and precision

Leaders constantly give directions, provide feedback, persuade, motivate, and negotiate. Mastering verbal communication means choosing the right words, using the appropriate tone, pace, and volume, and being skillful with pauses. When you get it right, you'll be able to turn monologues into meaningful connections. The key to effective verbal communication is clarity and precision. Let's look at some techniques for developing clear, concise speech, and understanding the impact of tone, pace, and volume.

- **Organize your thoughts** Before speaking, take a moment to organize your thoughts. Identify your main point and any supporting ideas. Having a mental blueprint will guide your speech and prevent you from going off-track.
- **Keep it simple** Use simple language, ensure your vocabulary is appropriate for your audience, and avoid jargon. The goal is to convey your message effectively, not show off your linguistic prowess.
- **Be specific** Generalizations can lead to misinterpretations. Being specific and detailed in what you say leaves less room for misunderstanding.
- **Use visual aids** Depending on the circumstances, incorporate diagrams, tables, charts, or illustrations to clarify complex ideas, and make it easy to remember key points.
- **Practice active listening** It is essential to listen carefully to your team's responses or queries, so you can understand their perspective and tailor your message accordingly.
- **Encourage questions** Questions can reveal areas of confusion or ambiguity, so be patient in addressing them.

The influence of tone, pace, and volume

While we may carefully choose words that express our thoughts, *how* we say them adds another layer of meaning. Tone, pace, and volume can convey emotions, attitudes, and conviction more vividly than our words alone.

- **Tone** Vocal tone can express a range of emotions, from joy and enthusiasm to anger or disappointment. A flat monotone may suggest boredom or disinterest, whereas a friendly, relaxed tone can put people at ease and invite open communication.
- **Pace** The speed, or pace, at which you speak determines how easy it is to follow what you are saying. Speaking too fast can make you appear nervous, or rushed, whereas speaking too slowly can make you sound dull. A moderate speaking pace, with pauses in the right places, is the most effective.
- **Volume** Adjust your volume to suit the situation and the audience. Speaking too softly can make you sound unsure or timid, whereas a booming voice can seem aggressive. The right level will help convey your intensity and conviction.

Imagine you are giving feedback to a team member. If you mutter a quick "well done", in a monotone, at low volume, the message might come across as insincere or unenthusiastic. But when the same words are said in a warm tone, at a relaxed pace, with appropriate volume, they exude genuine praise and encouragement.

Communication styles

Great communicators identify the communication styles of those around them and adapt their approach to match. Let's examine the four common communication styles.

- **Passive** Because they don't want to risk offending others, passive communicators tend to avoid expressing their opinions and feelings. On the surface, they might seem agreeable, but they often harbor resentment.

- **Aggressive** They tend to express their own opinions and feelings strongly, often disregarding what others have to say. They dominate conversations and can come across as intimidating or disrespectful.
- **Passive-aggressive** These individuals tend to express opinions and feelings indirectly, often resorting to sarcasm, backhanded compliments, or avoidance.
- **Assertive** They express their opinions and feelings directly and respectfully, while acknowledging other peoples' right to their own opinions and feelings. They foster open, honest communication and encourage feedback. This is the most effective communication style.

Understanding different communication styles can help you address individual team members. For example, you may have to use open-ended questions to get passive individuals to express their opinions. With aggressive individuals, you might need to adopt active listening and practice assertiveness to prevent one-sided conversations. Addressing indirect or hidden messages directly may foster healthier communication with passive-aggressive personalities. On the other hand, maintaining an open, two-way communication style may work best with assertive individuals.

> Communication styles are shaped by individual personality types and cultural contexts.

Communication styles are shaped by individual personality types and cultural contexts. Some people prefer direct, concise communication, whereas others appreciate more thoughtful conversations. Some are comfortable with talking, whereas others prefer written communication.

Understanding individual preferences will help you adapt your communications for maximum effectiveness. The personality style models described in Golden Star 3 will help you align your own communication style with your team members' personalities and communication preferences.

Feedback and constructive criticism

Positive feedback and constructive criticism play a role in improving performance by pushing individuals to reach their highest potential. They provide impetus for forward momentum, and sound a warning against possible missteps that might hinder progress. Handled with care, they can be powerful tools for fostering growth and strengthening relationships.

How to give feedback

- **Focus** Concentrate on specific aspects of performance or behavior. This avoids the ambiguity and potential hostility of generalized criticism.
- **Maintain balance** Don't only make negative comments. Feedback should include positive reinforcement, such as acknowledging something that was done well.
- **Offer suggestions** Provide practical suggestions for improvement. Don't just identify the problem; as a leader, you need to indicate your willingness to help resolve it.
- **Don't delay** Feedback should be given promptly, while the relevant details remain fresh, and suggested changes might still be able to resolve the issue.
- **Repeat the action** Giving regular feedback can lead to incremental improvement, which is beneficial for personal growth and development.

Effective feedback models

Popular models for giving feedback include SBI, STAR, and COBS. The SBI model (Situation, Behavior, Impact) sets out the situation where the behavior occurred, details the specific behavior, and explains the impact of that behavior. The STAR model (Situation, Task, Action, Result), which is often used in job interviews, can be adapted for feedback. It describes the situation or task, the action taken, and the result achieved. The COBS model (Context, Observation, Behavior, Suggestion) is a systematic way to structure feedback, from setting out the context, to stating the observation, focusing on the behavior, and suggesting improvements.

CARES feedback model

I developed the CARES model (Context, Action, Result, Effect, Solution), with the goal of promoting balanced discussions by combining objectivity with empathy. While it is primarily a tool for addressing identified problems, it can also be used to foster growth and development of individual team members. Putting the focus on specific behaviors, outcomes, and solutions, the model enables leaders to give feedback that is constructive, actionable, and empathic. The model taps into the frontal lobes of the brain, which are responsible for problem-solving and decision-making, as well as the limbic system, which governs our emotional responses.

With consistent use, the CARES model will become intuitive, and you will find it easier to give feedback that is helpful. However, bear in mind that every feedback session is unique, and leaders should adjust their approach to the individual and the situation. Always allow empathy, understanding, and respect to guide the feedback process.

- **Context** Accurately define the situation or event. An impartial description allows the individual to visualize the context in which the behavior occurred. This step is crucial for ensuring that feedback is grounded in a defined, relatable scenario.
- **Action** Clearly describe the behavior or action that prompted the feedback. Be objective and factual, and avoid any judgment or assumption about motivations. Focus on what was observed, detailing the action or behavior as it happened.
- **Result** Identify the outcomes that resulted from the action or behavior. What occurred as an immediate consequence, or subsequently? Detailing the repercussions provides clarity on the impact of the behavior, linking it directly to its outcomes.
- **Effect** What effect did the action or behavior have on the individual, the team, the project, or even the organization? Establishing the wider

implications and/or consequences helps the individual to understand the ripple effect of their actions.

- **Solution** Provide solutions that are practical and constructive. This might require the individual to modify behavior patterns, or focus on specific areas for improvement. Be supportive and offer suggestions to help them avoid similar issues in the future.

CARES FEEDBACK MODEL

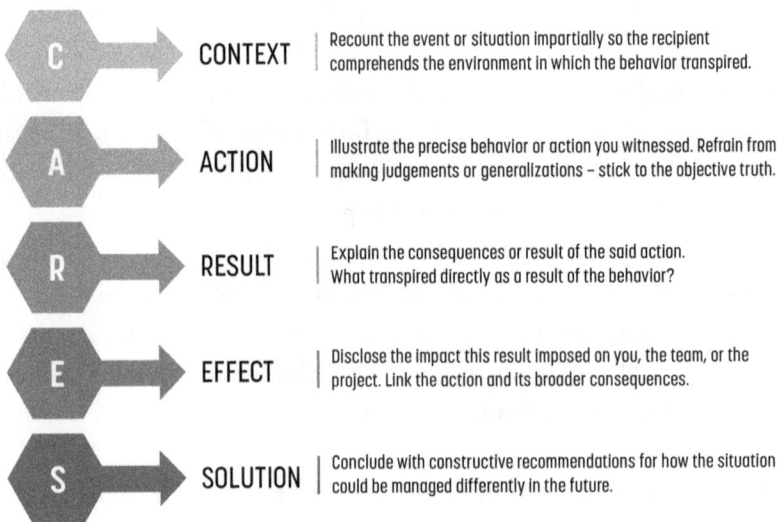

C	**CONTEXT**	Recount the event or situation impartially so the recipient comprehends the environment in which the behavior transpired.
A	**ACTION**	Illustrate the precise behavior or action you witnessed. Refrain from making judgements or generalizations – stick to the objective truth.
R	**RESULT**	Explain the consequences or result of the said action. What transpired directly as a result of the behavior?
E	**EFFECT**	Disclose the impact this result imposed on you, the team, or the project. Link the action and its broader consequences.
S	**SOLUTION**	Conclude with constructive recommendations for how the situation could be managed differently in the future.

Delivering constructive criticism

Constructive criticism encourages individuals to reassess their attitudes, and makes them more receptive to change. Because it highlights both personal strengths and weaknesses, leaders should suggest areas for improvement, or opportunities for growth, rather than focus solely on pointing out faults. Being given clear expectations can result in improved job performance and productivity. It takes practice and tact to deliver constructive criticism in a formal context, such as a performance review. However, when done with care, it can enhance mutual trust and respect, setting the stage for success.

Here are some ways to give constructive criticism:

- **Create a safe space** Meet with the individual in a closed meeting room, or a setting where they may be more receptive to feedback.
- **Empathize** Remember that your aim is to assist the individual, not make things more difficult for them.
- **Utilize "I" statements** Frame your comments as perceptions ("I think..."), not as direct accusations, or questioning of motives.
- **Be precise** Outline the specific issue or problem, and its implications for the team.
- **Center on actions, not the individual** Focus on the undesirable action or behavior, not personal traits.
- **Propose solutions** Suggest ways to resolve the identified problems.
- **Encourage dialogue** Allow the individual to respond without interrupting them, and listen to what they have to say.

STORY IN PRACTICE

Communicating with care

Lee Oliver, the regional manager of a company that operated upmarket retirement estates, was responsible for ensuring that the properties were well-run and profitable. When he noticed that one property had a few vacancies, but no names on the waiting list, he arranged a meeting with Anne Fontaine, the on-site manager, to discuss the situation.

Arriving with time to spare, he walked around the property, and was surprised by what he saw. Although the pool and gym were open, both were empty. The hair salon was closed, and a sign on the door indicated it was only open for a few hours twice a week. A sign at the front desk indicated that the shuttle bus to the nearest town made just two trips a week. Noticing Anne talking to the receptionist, he heard her say that the activities manager had just cancelled an activity that was due to start within the hour. This fell short of the company's standards, and was not what the residents were paying for.

Sitting in Anne's office a few minutes later, Lee began by asking why the hair salon and the shuttle bus had such limited operating times. In both cases, the answer was the same: The stylist and bus driver were both contract workers, with other jobs outside the estate. In response to a question about why there was no back-up plan in the event of a cancelled activity, Anne said that the activities manager had been experiencing health problems recently, which had curtailed the event, and meant she was often unavailable at short notice. When pressed further, Anne was unable to say why a temporary solution had not been implemented.

Lee realized he needed a constructive feedback session with Anne. After evaluating some options, he decided on the CARES feedback model. He recognized that Anne's communication style was quite passive, so he planned his conversation with that in mind.

The following week, Lee began by outlining the context of the meeting. Keeping his tone neutral, he said to Anne: "This property is underperforming. The financials are consistently lower than similar properties. We also have a high number of vacancies, but no-one wanting to move in. I'm sure you understand that something has to be done."

Anne nodded, but Lee wanted to get her involved in the conversation. Remembering that passive communicators respond best to open-ended questions, he asked: "What do you think is the reason for the poor results?" Anne was silent for a moment and then said, "We can't get tenants." "How good are we at retaining tenants?" Lee asked. Anne sighed and said, "Not very good." "Why is that?" Lee asked gently. Anne had no answer.

Moving on to the action step of the model, Lee reminded Anne of what he had witnessed the previous week. "That level of service is not up to our standards," he said. "And I've since learned that activities at this property are very sporadic."

As Anne started to make excuses for her staff, Lee interrupted her. "Anne, the facts are clear. The salon should be open five days a week. The shuttle bus should run three times a day. There should be a variety of activities throughout the week. That is our standard. Yet we are nowhere near that level of service because, from what I've observed, your employees seem to set their own hours."

Next, Lee pointed out the potential result or outcome. Using open-ended questions, he asked Anne whether she thought the tenants were getting value for their money. "I know some are not happy with the lack of facilities," she responded. "If you were them, what would you do about it?" Lee asked. Looking out of her office window, Anne said quietly, "Leave."

The conversation shifted to the impact the staffing situation was having. Lee told Anne, "If we cannot retain tenants, we won't be profitable. And if they are unhappy, our reputation suffers, because personal referrals play a big part in attracting new tenants. A downward spiral of tenants leaving and not being replaced could result in the company closing the estate."

"And yet," Lee said, now ready to offer a solution, "I believe the situation can be resolved." He felt it was important to make this point: Anne's demeanor told him that she felt utterly defeated. "This is a beautiful property in a gorgeous location. People should want to live here! The change must begin with you. I admire your concern for your employees, but your objective is to meet the company's set standards. If this property closes, everybody loses their job, including you. You need to explain to your employees that if they cannot meet the required standards, they will be asked to resign. The conversations won't be easy, but you must be firm. I'll help you prepare, and the company can send you on courses to learn how to manage change and be a more successful leader. Together, I know we can turn the property around."

In the following months, with support from Lee and the company, Anne made progress. Consultations resulted in some retrenchments, resignations and retirements, but a contingent of enthusiastic new employees soon upgraded the services and amenities. The shuttle bus ran regularly, the salon offered a full range of hair and beauty treatments, and the events manager revitalized the program of daily and weekly activities. Throughout the period of transition, Anne learned how to become more assertive in her dealings with her staff.

The story of Lee Oliver and Anne Fontaine illustrates the power of well-researched and well-structured feedback. Lee's open-ended questioning, and his ability to interpret non-verbal gestures, were tailored to Anne's passive communication style, and made her more willing to recognize her role in the original problem. Mastering communication skills is vital for leaders; if you can't lead, others can't follow.

Presentation skills

As a team leader, you may have to give short presentations, make a speech in celebration of a milestone, or introduce a new team member to a group. Most people find speaking in public intimidating, and try their best to get out of it. Here are some tips for ensuring that you can approach public speaking with confidence:

- **Be prepared** Write down what you want to say and review it a few times beforehand. Practice at home, or in a secluded place, so you can speak the words, as you would in the presentation. Saying words in your head is not the same as speaking them out loud. You'll be surprised at how your vocal tone and pitch changes when you stand up and speak.
- **Be relevant** Presentations usually have a specific objective, such as sharing the latest sales figures, or outlining the goals for the next quarter. Staying on point makes it easier for your audience to remember the key facts of your presentation.
- **Time it right** Most presentations are short. Keep to the main points, and don't be tempted to detour from them. This is especially relevant if people are standing, as at a company cocktail party, for example.
- **Practice using visual aids** If your presentation involves audio-visual aids, make sure you have practiced with them. You need to know how many slides you can incorporate in the given time and how long to display each one.
- **Know your equipment** Technical competence is another aspect of preparation. Your audience doesn't want to watch you struggling to synch your laptop with the AV link, or hear email alerts pinging in the background! If you are using a microphone, check the sound levels, and know where the mute button is.

There may be occasions when your presentation skills are put to the test by having to speak to a large group, in a bigger venue. In this case, you'll need to up your game. To learn more about public speaking, turn to the Bonus Star at the back of the book.

Asking questions

The first part of this Golden Star covered listening and speaking. Now, we turn our attention to questions and stories. By asking the "right" questions, leaders can obtain specific information, and come to understand their team members in a more profound way. Telling stories enables leaders to convey messages that will be remembered.

Questioning is an essential communications skill. Questions create space for dialogue. They promote inquiry and encourage curiosity. Good leaders use questions to gather information, or gain insights into people and problems. Careful questioning can challenge assumptions, and guide individuals or teams towards discovery, understanding, and innovative thinking.

By making an inquiring mindset part of their communication style, leaders can stimulate deeper thinking, foster engagement, and facilitate problem-solving and decision-making. This requires leaders to be receptive to new insights and perspectives, comfortable with not having all the answers, and to accept that others may have ideas, knowledge, and experience they lack.

Here are some examples of how asking the right questions can guide your thinking:

> Careful questioning can challenge assumptions, and guide individuals or teams towards discovery, understanding, and innovative thinking.

- **Understand** Ask "what–when–where" questions to gather information or gain insights that you can use to understand others' perspectives.
- **Guide** Asking, "How do you feel about this option?" allows you to direct your team's focus, and facilitate learning and discovery.
- **Challenge** Use "why" or "how" questions to stimulate critical thinking, challenge assumptions, or generate new ideas.
- **Connect** Show interest in and respect for individual views or opinions by asking "What do you think?" Connecting with others helps build stronger relationships.
- **Decide** Questions such as "What would you do?" ensure that everyone's input is considered, and facilitate decision-making.

By framing questions carefully, you can guide the conversation and maintain focus. Take time to think about what you want to achieve, and plan your questioning session with an end goal in mind. This will enable you to select the right type of questions for the situation.

- **Be clear and concise** Keep questions simple, and ensure they align with the purpose of the conversation or discussion. Avoid ambiguity.
- **Start broad, then narrow down** Begin with open-ended questions to get the conversation going, then use probing questions to obtain more specific information.
- **Encourage thinking** Frame questions in a way that stimulates thinking and requires answers that go beyond just "yes' or "no" responses.

Different situations call for different types of questions:

- **Open-ended questions** These encourage dialogue and exploration. They allow respondents to elaborate on their thoughts and share them freely. Examples include "What do you think about ...?" and "How did you come to that conclusion?"
- **Closed-ended questions** These are best when you require a straightforward answer, need to confirm facts, or want a specific, usually short, response. Examples include, "Have you finished the report?" and "Will you attend the meeting?"
- **Probing questions** These delve more deeply into a topic, or examine a response to a previous question. They clarify details, explore underlying issues, and seek reasons. Examples include, "Can you elaborate on ...?" and "What makes you say that?"

Strategic questioning asks the right questions at the right time in order to understand or discover things, generate ideas, solve problems, or initiate further action.
- **Diagnostic questions** "Can you tell me more about this?"
- **Exploratory questions** "Do you have any suggestions on how to resolve this matter?"

- **Prioritizing questions** "How important do you think this is?"
- **Action questions** "What is your plan?"

Questions that challenge assumptions allow leaders to consider all options. They can also stimulate innovative problem-solving.

- **Identify assumptions** "What assumptions are we making here?"
- **Challenge assumptions** "What if our assumption is wrong?"
- **Explore alternatives** "What other possibilities could there be?"

Use questions based on dialogue and consensus to facilitate collaborative decision-making.

- **Solicit opinions** "What do you think we should do?"
- **Explore pros and cons** "What are the benefits and drawbacks of pursuing this option?"
- **Build consensus** "Can we all agree on this?"

Questions directed towards personal feelings can help resolve issues, manage conflict, or ease difficult conversations.

- **Seek understanding** "Can you help me understand why you feel this way?"
- **Acknowledge feelings** "How did that make you feel?"
- **Facilitate problem-solving** "How do you think we can resolve this?"

Follow-up questions give leaders the opportunity to dig deeper, clarify their own understanding, and encourage others to expand their thinking.

- **Probe** "Can you elaborate on that?"
- **Clarify** "What do you mean by that?"
- **Explore** "What would be the implications of that?"

Four models for effective questioning

Widely recognized questioning models include Bloom's Taxonomy, Grow, and The 5 Whys. To them, I've added my own Craft model.

Bloom's Taxonomy

Developed in the 1950s by educational psychologist Benjamin Bloom and his colleagues, this hierarchical model classifies learning objectives into six levels, from confirming basic facts to evaluating ideas or concepts. Incorporating Bloom's model into your questioning strategy will help you frame questions in a systematic way to achieve a desirable outcome.

1. **Remember** Confirm that specific information or facts are recognized and understood, or that the relevant details can be located or recalled.
   - "Can you list the main components of our project plan?"
   - "Do you know where to locate our company policy on flexible work hours?"

2. **Understand** Asking individuals to explain or interpret information in their own words is a good indicator of how well they understand it.
   - "Can you explain why we need to meet this deadline?"
   - "What is the objective of our new marketing strategy?"

3. **Apply** Ask individuals to apply facts, concepts or knowledge to a problem or situation.
   - "Will our problem-solving protocol resolve the issue that we are currently facing?"
   - "What aspects of our previous marketing campaign can we apply to the new project?'

4. **Analyze** Break down the components of an issue and explore the connections between them.
   - "What trends can we identify from our latest customer feedback?"
   - "If we go ahead with this initiative, will there be any impact on other departments?"

5. **Evaluate** Use questions to stimulate critical thinking, and judge the value of information or ideas before proposing alternative solutions.
   - "Based on our team's strengths and the project requirements, how should we structure our approach?"
   - "Can we synthesize feedback from our clients to come up with a new product idea?"

6. **Create** Consider how you can combine everything you've learned to come up with a new idea, product, or problem-solving solution.
   - "Based on what we know, what is our most likely route to a successful product?"
   - "What are the pros and cons of implementing this new software system?"

BLOOM'S TAXONOMY

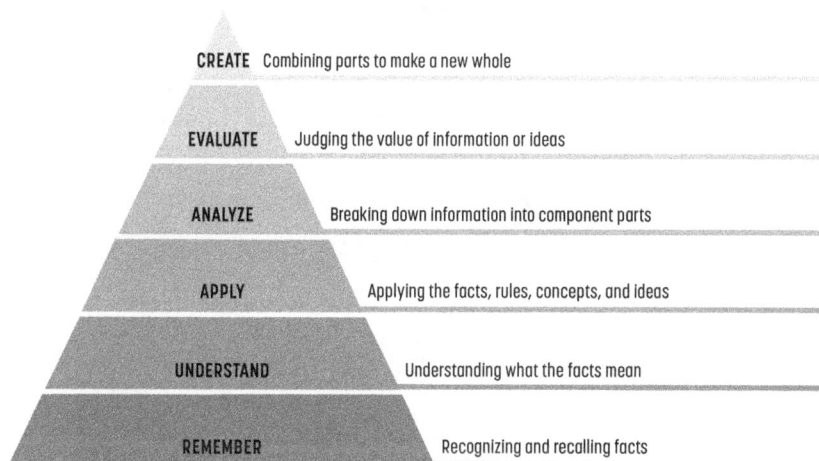

CREATE	Combining parts to make a new whole
EVALUATE	Judging the value of information or ideas
ANALYZE	Breaking down information into component parts
APPLY	Applying the facts, rules, concepts, and ideas
UNDERSTAND	Understanding what the facts mean
REMEMBER	Recognizing and recalling facts

The GROW model

Leaders can use the structured approach of the GROW model to facilitate productive conversations. Created in the 1980s by Sir John Whitmore, Graham Alexander, and Alan Fine, GROW (Goal, Reality, Options, Way Forward) is a popular model for coaching, goal-setting, problem-solving,

183

and performance improvement. Whether you are coaching an individual team member, or leading a group planning session, the GROW model will help provide clarity, and improve communication.

1. **Goal** Set SMART goals (Specific, Measurable, Achievable, Relevant, Time-bound), and ask questions that help team members define their objectives and goals.
   - "What would you like to achieve in this project/task/role?"
   - "Can you define your goal in specific and measurable terms?"
   - "How relevant is success to you in this situation?"

2. **Reality** Establish the current situation (reality). This includes understanding any challenges or obstacles that stand in the way, and finding out what resources are available to overcome them.
   - "Where are we now with respect to your goal?"
   - "What challenges or obstacles are you currently facing?"
   - "What resources do you have at your disposal?"

3. **Options** Explore possible strategies to reach the defined goal. Use open-ended questions to encourage creative thinking and problem-solving.
   - "What strategies could we explore to reach your goal?"
   - "If there were no constraints, what options might you consider?"
   - "How can you leverage your available resources?"

4. **Will Do** Create an action plan, outlining tasks that will move the individual or team towards the goal. Ensure the plan is realistic and achievable, and ask questions that signal commitment.
   - "What specific steps will you take to achieve your goal?"
   - "What potential challenges might you encounter, and how will you address them?"
   - "When and how will you start implementing this plan?"

THE GROW MODEL

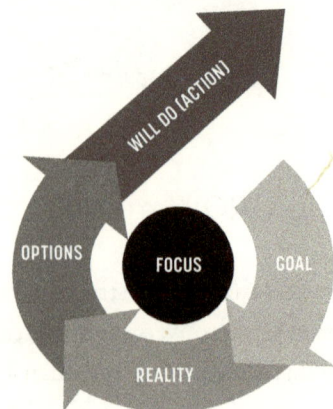

The 5 Whys model

Developed by Sakichi Toyoda, the founder of Toyota Industries, as a technique for solving problems, the 5 Whys model is based on cause and effect. The goal is to identify the *cause* of an issue by repeatedly asking "Why?" in order to systematically reveal the *effect* (impact) arising from the issue. Because the model embodies a culture of continuous improvement and critical thinking, leaders can use it to guide their teams past symptom-level thinking towards the real cause of an issue. "Why" questioning, also known as root cause analysis, encourages curiosity, critical thinking, and problem-solving, and requires teams to address core issues, not just put out fires.

1. **Identify the problem** Begin by agreeing on the specific issue. Start with a declarative statement, such as: "We missed our sales target for the third consecutive quarter."

2. **Ask "Why?"** Introduce the first "Why?" question as you start to uncover the problem.
   Question: "Why did we miss our sales target?"
   Possible answer: "Because our key product was out of stock for more than a month."

3. **Probe deeper** By repeating "Why?" in response to each answer, you probe deeper into the cause and effect of the problem. Each new question should derive from the answer to the previous "why."
   Question: "Why was our key product out of stock?"
   Possible answer: "There was a delay in production."
   Question: "Why was there a delay in production?"
   Possible answer: "There was a supply chain disruption."
   Question: "Why was there a supply chain disruption?"
   Possible answer: "Our only supplier couldn't fulfill the order on time."

4. **Identify the cause** After several iterations of "why?", the cause of the problem will be revealed. This is typically a process or systemic issue that can be addressed to prevent the problem from recurring.

Example: "Our reliance on a single supplier led to a disruption in the supply chain and subsequent delay in production."

5. **Implement solutions** Once the cause has been identified, the team can create and implement a solution. As a leader, you should monitor the situation to verify that the problem has been solved.
Example: "Let's diversify our supplier base to reduce the risk of supply chain disruption in the future. Regularly checking our sales figures will ensure we remain on target."

THE 5 WHYS MODEL

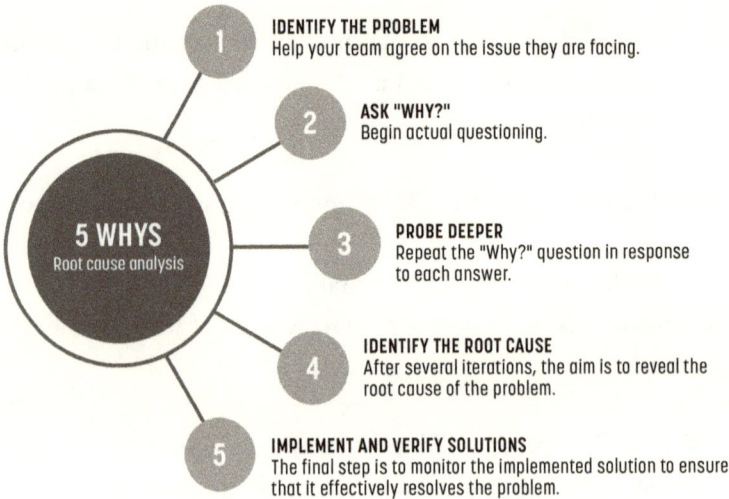

IDENTIFY THE PROBLEM
Help your team agree on the issue they are facing.

ASK "WHY?"
Begin actual questioning.

5 WHYS
Root cause analysis

PROBE DEEPER
Repeat the "Why?" question in response to each answer.

IDENTIFY THE ROOT CAUSE
After several iterations, the aim is to reveal the root cause of the problem.

IMPLEMENT AND VERIFY SOLUTIONS
The final step is to monitor the implemented solution to ensure that it effectively resolves the problem.

The CRAFT model

The CRAFT model, which I designed, integrates the principles of effective questioning with neuroscience. It paves the way for new insights, better understanding, and collaborative problem-solving by facilitating an environment of openness, and promoting a culture of critical thinking, and continuous improvement. Incorporating neuroscientific principles, the model's structured approach optimizes the power of questioning by aligning it with how the brain processes information. Neuroscience tells us that effective questioning activates specific areas of the brain, including those that govern cognition (understanding) and emotional engagement.

CRAFT stands for Clarify, Reason, Analyze, Focus, and Transform. The prefrontal cortex, which processes complex information, helps us clarify issues and objectives.[6] Reasoning activates areas of the brain involved in logical thinking and decision-making. Analyzing encourages deeper cognitive processing, and activates regions of the brain linked to problem-solving and critical thinking.[7] Focusing harnesses the brain's attention networks. Finally, the transformative aspect of CRAFT engages the brain's higher-order processing capacity to reflect on learning, and apply insights to future scenarios, fostering a growth mindset and neuroplasticity.[8]

Begin by creating a brief scenario that outlines a problem or a situation that requires decisions to be made. As you apply the model, write down the answers and insights you obtain.

1. **Clarify** Ask probing questions to clarify your understanding of the situation. (This aligns with "Current Reality" in the GROW model, and "Understand" and "Remember" in Bloom's Taxonomy.)
    - "Can you describe the situation in more detail?"
    - "What challenges are we facing?"
    - "What is the main issue here?"

2. **Reason** Examine the reasoning (thought processes) or causes behind any actions or decisions. Break down the details to help identify motives or causes. (This aligns with the "Why" questions in the 5 Whys, and "Apply" in Bloom's Taxonomy.)
    - "Why did we decide to take this approach?"
    - "What are the underlying reasons for this situation?"
    - "What factors led us to this point?"

3. **Analyze** Assess the situation by exploring all options, and consider possible outcomes. (This aligns with "Options" in the GROW model, and "Analyze" in Bloom's Taxonomy.)
    - "What are the likely outcomes if we follow this course of action?"
    - "What are the alternatives?"
    - "How does this situation relate to our past experiences?"

4. **Focus** Determine the preferred outcome and outline the steps needed to get there. By considering all the information, you should be able formulate a way forward. (This aligns with "Will Do" in the GROW model, and "Evaluate" in Bloom's Taxonomy.)
   - "Which option is most aligned with our goals?"
   - "What will be our immediate next steps?"
   - "What resources will we need?"

5. **Transform** Reflect on what you have learned. Using insights gained from the exercise, consider the implications for the future. (This aligns with "Create" in Bloom's Taxonomy.)
   - "What have we learned from this process?"
   - "How can we apply these insights to future situations?"
   - "What changes can we make to prevent this from recurring?"

THE CRAFT MODEL

C   **CLARIFY**   "Can you describe the situation in more detail?"
"What challenges are we facing?"
"What is the main issue here?"

R   **REASON**   "Why did we decide to take this approach?"
"What are the underlying reasons for this challenge?"
"What factors led us to this point?"

A   **ANALYZE**   "What are the potential consequences if we continue on this path?"
"What are the alternatives?"
"How does this situation relate to past experiences?"

F   **FOCUS**   "Among the options, which is the most aligned with our goals?"
"What will be our immediate next steps?"
"What resources will we need?"

T   **TRANSFORM**   "What have we learned from this process?"
"How can we apply these insights to future situations?"
"What changes can we make to prevent this issue from recurring?"

Telling stories

You learn things by asking questions. You convey things by telling stories. Stories are a powerful medium for communicating important information or essential messages. Perhaps the best illustration of this is the stories we tell children. Whether they are fairy tales, fables, or fact, children's stories all carry a message. They educate, inform, and entertain and, in doing so, they teach valuable lessons about life, emotions, behavior and attitudes.

As a team leader, you can harness the power of storytelling to engage with your team members in a way that a simple stating of facts could never accomplish. As with presentation skills and public speaking, the art of telling a good story comes more naturally to some people than to others. If you often find yourself at the center of a group, regaling them with tales of this and that, you are probably a natural storyteller. If this is not you, don't worry. With practice, even the shyest individual can learn to deliver the right story at the right moment.

The key is to know your audience and stick to the topic. Start simple, perhaps by saying a few words about a colleague on a special occasion. Do your homework beforehand, and discover something about them that is not well known, but suits the moment. If it is something you witnessed, an easy starting point is "I remember when ...". Sharing an anecdote is always easier when you are among colleagues, and someone else is ready to chip in with another story, and another. Soon, everyone is "telling stories" without realizing it!

If you like listening to other people's stories, you probably already have more storytelling skills than you realize. Begin listening more intently, and focus on their delivery, pace, and how they adapt their stories to suit the occasion, and the listeners. The same story might be told very differently on a night out with the boys, than at a family gathering!

If you have children, listen to their stories. Young imaginations know no bounds, and if you pay attention to what they are saying, you'll find yourself asking "So what happened next?" or "But why did she do that?" That's the power of storytelling!

For more on how to use storytelling in your leadership practice, turn to the Bonus Star at the end of the book.

SELF-REFLECTION PIT STOP

Scan the QR code or visit drtomdreyer.com/tools to download your e-toolkit.

Communication mastery check-in

On your leadership journey, you need to pause every now and then to take stock of where you are now, and where you are heading. Use this pit stop to assess your communication skills, and develop a personalized action plan to help you improve.

1. **Understanding the communication process** Reflect on your understanding of the entire communication process. Are you clear on the roles of sender and receiver, and the nature of the message? Are you making the most of your opportunities to communicate effectively, or can you do more?

2. **Active listening** Rate your active listening skills on a scale of 1–10. What practices do you have in place to ensure you're fully present when someone else is speaking? Can you recall a recent conversation where you demonstrated active listening? If not, what distracted you?

3. **Non-verbal communication** During your interactions with your team, are your body language, tone of voice, and facial expressions congruent with your spoken words? How can you better align your non-verbal cues with your messages?

4. **Presentation skills** How do you feel about your presentation skills? Are you confident about speaking in front of others, or does it create anxiety? Do you adapt your approach to your audience, and can you accommodate adjustments to your presentation time? What steps can you take to improve these areas?

5. **Questioning skills** Think about the last team meeting or one-on-one conversation you had. Did you ask meaningful questions that fostered critical thinking and dialogue? What questioning models can you incorporate into your leadership practice?

6. **Storytelling** How often do you use storytelling in your communications? Can you recall a recent instance where a story effectively engaged your team members or other stakeholders? What elements of your storytelling can you strengthen?

7. **Set SMART goals** Use SMART goals to improve your communication skills. For example: "Over the next three months, I will share a relevant story or anecdote at the start of team meetings to engage everyone, and give them a memorable take-away."

Mastering communication takes time. Keep practicing, remain open to feedback, and celebrate your progress. Golden Star 7 examined the principles that underpin effective communication, from developing listening skills and decoding non-verbal cues, to giving feedback. We have also explored the power of questioning, and considered how storytelling can help get your message across. Each lesson includes tools and insights that will improve your skills and help you communicate better.

Endnotes

1   Sakai, K. L. (2008). Language acquisition and brain development. *Science*, 310(5749), 815-819.]

2   Adolphs, R. (2010). Conceptual challenges and directions for social neuroscience. *Neuron*, 65(6), 752-767.

3   Hsu, M., Bhatt, M., Adolphs, R., Tranel, D., & Camerer, C. F. (2005). Neural systems responding to degrees of uncertainty in human decision-making. *Science*, 310(5754), 1680-1683.

4   Kosfeld, M., Heinrichs, M., Zak, P. J., Fischbacher, U., & Fehr, E. (2005). Oxytocin increases trust in humans. *Nature*, 435(7042), 673-676.

5   Iacoboni, M. (2009). Imitation, empathy, and mirror neurons. *Annual Review of Psychology*, 60, 653-670.

6   Sakai, K. L. (2008). Language acquisition and brain development. *Science*, 310(5749), 815-819.

7   Heekeren, H. R., Marrett, S., Bandettini, P. A., & Ungerleider, L. G. (2004). A general mechanism for perceptual decision-making in the human brain. *Nature*, 431(7010), 859-862.

8   Davidson, R. J., & McEwen, B. S. (2012). Social influences on neuroplasticity: Stress and interventions to promote well-being. *Nature Neuroscience*, 15(5), 689-695.

GOLDEN STAR

RESILIENCE, ADAPTABILITY, AND TRANSFORMATION

In a world where the only constant is change, the rhythm of progress beats at an increasingly rapid pace. This Golden Star looks at two skills that are often undervalued: resilience and adaptability. Cultivating these skills will serve you well on your leadership journey, and help you cope with the ever-present realities of a volatile, uncertain, complex, and ambiguous world.

Embracing resilience and adaptability

Resilience enables you to rebound from adversity, disappointment, or failure. It is the ability to persevere in the face of challenges, and the capacity to endure ongoing pressure. Resilience is the unwavering tenacity that enables leaders to overcome setbacks, and emerge stronger, wiser, and more determined.

> Resilience enables leaders to overcome setbacks, and emerge stronger, wiser and more determined.

Adaptability represents an agility of mind that enables us to respond swiftly and effectively to changing situations. It's about being flexible in our approach, and pivoting in response to an unexpected event. In leadership, it is also about coping with evolving strategies or changes of direction, and transforming obstacles into opportunities. Resilience and adaptability are no longer optional. Today's leaders require these traits to guide their teams through uncertainty and change. To lead is to adapt, and to endure is to be resilient.

Before you can develop resilience in your team, you need to cultivate personal resilience.

- **Make time for self-care** Attend to your physical wellbeing. Exercise, healthy eating, and quality sleep are not just feel-good choices; they're brain hacks. Developing these habits boosts memory and enhances decision-making and brainpower, thanks to increased cell growth and improved blood flow.[1] This, in turn, fuels the resilience, adaptability, and sharp thinking that leaders need to navigate challenges and inspire their team. Make self-care your leadership superpower. Nourishing your brain will unlock your best self.

- **Practice mindfulness** Investing a few minutes each day to cultivate this neuroscience-backed superpower is sure to pay off. Meditation rewires your brain for enhanced emotional self-regulation and increased resilience.[2] It can also lower stress levels. Mindfulness strengthens the regions of the brain that manage emotions, helping you to bounce back from setbacks, and stay calm under pressure.
- **Foster a positive outlook** Be optimistic, and acknowledge that change and adversity are part of life. Recognize that adversity frequently sparks growth, while setbacks can create a path for fresh opportunities.
- **Nurture strong relationships** Establish and nurture robust relationships in all areas of your life. When tackling challenges, you'll be able to turn to those with whom you have a strong bond to provide support, or offer advice or an alternative viewpoint.
- **Embrace continuous learning** Be receptive to new experiences, and view challenges as opportunities for growth. Becoming more resilient will enhance your leadership capabilities.

Building a resilient team

A step-by-step approach will give team members time to fully embrace each stage as they discover their personal levels of resilience.

1. **Promote a supportive environment** Encourage open communication and mutual support among team members. Let them know that while it can be acceptable to get things wrong, failures should be used as learning opportunities.
2. **Encourage problem-solving** Allow your team to confront challenges, and devise creative solutions to problems. Strengthening their problem-solving skills will boost resilience.
3. **Recognition** Acknowledge team members' efforts to persevere in the face of challenges. When they see that resilient behavior is recognized, it can inspire them to become more resilient themselves.
4. **Provide resources** Ensure your team has access to any resources and training they might need to help them manage workplace stress and pressure more effectively.

5. **Demonstrate resilience** As a leader, you should personify resilience. Being resilient yourself can inspire your team to emulate such behavior.

Adaptability quotient

The adaptability quotient (AQ) is a way to measure individual (or organizational) capacity to adapt to new or changing circumstances. It gauges how effectively a leader can unlearn outdated methods, embrace new ways of thinking or acting, shift perspectives, and adjust an existing action plan in response to change.

General intelligence (IQ) and emotional intelligence (EQ) have long been standard-bearers of leadership success, but in a world of persistent uncertainty, AQ is the new frontrunner. Being adaptable can boost success, improve job security, and make it easier to adopt new technology. Leaders who fail to adopt AQ risk falling behind in their efforts to keep pace with rapid change.

The ARC-EQ model

Agility, Resilience, Curiosity, and Emotional intelligence (EQ), are the elements of my own adaptability model, which is based on neuroscience principles. The model is both cyclical and perpetual, with each element supporting the others in a continuous feedback loop.

Neuroscience shows how these elements, which are deeply rooted in brain function, are essential for adaptability. Agility, which is associated with the executive functions of the prefrontal cortex, is pivotal for adaptive decision-making.[3] Resilience is linked to the brain's stress response and neuroplasticity mechanisms.[4] Curiosity stimulates the brain's reward system, and aligns with the desire for continuous learning.[5] Emotional intelligence is tied to the limbic system, which is crucial for empathic and socially aware leadership.[6]

ARC-EQ MODEL

A Agility	• Continuous learning plan • Pivot strategy worksheet • Innovation challenges
R Resilience	• Stress management • Positive affirmations • Reflection practice
C Curiosity	• Curiosity journal • Learning exchanges • Inquisitiveness exercises
EQ Emotional intelligence	• Self-assessment tools • Empathy exercises • Communication training

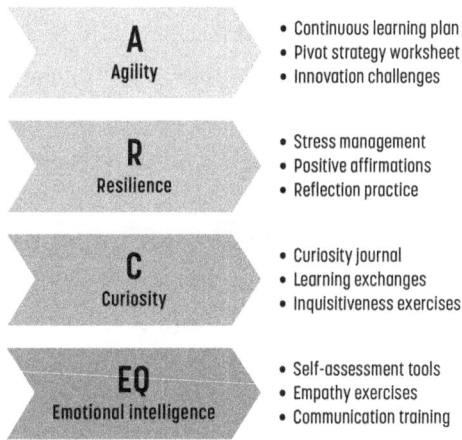

Implementing the ARC-EQ model

The ARC-EQ model incorporates practical exercises aimed at helping leaders improve their adaptability quotient. Implementing it allows leaders to develop their thinking and ability to lead effectively. Regular assessment, and a readiness to make strategic shifts based on feedback, will enable you to adapt to change with confidence and proficiency.

Agility Mental nimbleness, flexible thinking, and a proactive approach to decision-making are the hallmarks of an agile leader. These individuals welcome change, are receptive to fresh ideas, and can swiftly adjust to new circumstances. Agility can be nurtured through lifelong learning, acceptance of feedback, and cultivating a growth-oriented mindset.

- **Continuous learning** Identify any management skills that you feel need improvement. Set clear learning goals and allocate time for professional development so your leadership approach remains dynamic and current.

197

- **Strategic planning** Routinely assess your current strategies and adjust them as needed. Use formal worksheets or informal reviews to ensure that your strategy always aligns with the changing environment.
- **Innovation challenges** Stimulate innovation by conducting regular brainstorming sessions. Encouraging your team to come up with creative solutions will develop their problem-solving abilities.

Resilience Building resilience is the key to becoming adaptable. You can accomplish this by adopting a positive outlook, managing stress effectively, and reframing challenges as opportunities for growth. Resilient leaders have the capacity to overcome obstacles, and the ability to bounce back with robustness and insight.

- **Stress management** Breathing exercises, mindfulness meditation, and regular physical activity are all established techniques for sustaining a balanced lifestyle.
- **Positive affirmations** Performing daily self-affirmations that foster positivity will help you recover from setbacks.
- **Reflection practice** Consistently evaluate your experiences and acquired knowledge, and extract aspects that will help bolster your resilience.

Curiosity Leaders with a high AQ are inherently curious. They consistently challenge established norms, and seek to improve things. They have a passion for learning, are open to new experiences, and examine different viewpoints to broaden their understanding.

- **Curiosity journal** Maintain a journal to document new ideas, record queries, and capture learning experiences.
- **Learning exchanges** Coordinate sessions where team members can share their expertise, experiences, or lessons learned with others.
- **Inquisitiveness exercises** Encourage a culture of enquiry by asking open-ended questions about processes, strategies, or industry trends.

Emotional Intelligence A high EQ often goes hand-in-hand with a high AQ. Emotional intelligence amplifies a leader's self-awareness, self-control, motivation, empathy, and social capabilities, all of which are integral for adaptability. Leaders with a high EQ are able to regulate both their own emotions and those of their team, thus creating and sustaining a more adaptive and positive work environment.

- **Self-assessment tools** Use EQ self-assessment tools to identify your strengths, as well as any areas that require improvement.
- **Empathy exercises** Cultivate empathy by stepping into others' shoes, understanding their perspectives, and acknowledging their emotions.
- **Communication training** Attend and/or conduct regular training sessions or workshops aimed at enhancing communication, feedback delivery skills, and conflict resolution.

Leading your team through change

Change is a profound and persistent reality for organizations worldwide. It can emerge from a technological revolution, an unexpected global pandemic, political conflict, financial crisis, or shifts in market dynamics. It's like an unwelcome guest who shows up at your door and refuses to leave; you may not have invited it, but you have to deal with it.

> By providing clarity, direction, and support, leaders can help their teams successfully navigate change.

Today's leaders are expected to be change agents; individuals who don't just manage change, but drive it. Most people find change unsettling and disorienting. This is where leaders can make a difference. By providing clarity, direction, and support, leaders can help their teams successfully navigate change.

To become an effective change leader, you need to fulfill multiple roles, including strategist, mentor, communicator, and therapist. The strategist role involves envisioning the change and developing a robust plan. As a mentor, you provide the necessary support and guidance to team members during the change process. Being the communicator entails keeping the lines of communication open and ensuring your team understands the what, why, and how of the change. Finally, the therapist role requires you to empathize with your team, understand their emotions, and help them cope with the changes they are facing.

Leading through change means encouraging your team to view change not as a threat, but as an opportunity for growth and innovation. It also means creating a culture where flexibility, learning, and agility are recognized, valued and rewarded.

Your Adaptability Quotient equips you to be resilient in the face of adversity, agile and open to new ideas, and curious to explore the unfamiliar. Being emotionally intelligent allows you to understand and manage both your and others' emotions effectively. Remember, the goal is not just to survive change, but to thrive in it.

Understanding change

As we stand on the cusp of our journey towards understanding change, I am reminded of the ancient Greek philosopher, Heraclitus, who said: "The only thing that is constant is change." In today's fast-paced and dynamic business world, this holds true more than ever.

Change is a transition from a known present to an unknown future. While the unknown can often appear daunting and cloaked in uncertainty, it also brims with possibilities and opportunities. Change is not a one-size-fits-all phenomenon. It is multifaceted, and varies in its nature and scope. We can broadly categorize change into three types: developmental, transitional, and transformational.

1. **Developmental change** This is about doing what you are already doing, but better. It involves improvements to existing processes, practices, or performance standards. It's like upgrading from good to great.

2. **Transitional change** This is a shift from one state to another. Think of it as moving from old to new. Transitional change could involve

implementing a new technology system, launching a new product line, or restructuring an entire organization.

3. **Transformational change** This involves a fundamental shift in an organization's strategy, culture, or identity. We're talking about a metamorphosis here; like a caterpillar transforming into a butterfly.

Change can be driven by internal or external factors. Factors that drive internal change include new leadership, the launch of new products or withdrawal of old ones, or persistent failure to meet targets. Factors that drive external change include technological advancements, regulatory changes, or market dynamics.

Other ways that change can impact on organizations include new structures (through mergers, acquisitions, or downsizing), shifts in corporate culture, or adjustments to job roles or work flow. While some impacts will be challenging to navigate, change can also result in improved performance, increased innovation, and a stronger competitive advantage.

Emotions and change

Change can be an emotional roller coaster, giving rise to anything from fear and resistance to excitement and acceptance. As leaders, it is our responsibility to guide our teams through this journey, recognize their emotional reactions, and support them every step of the way.

Emotions make us human. They are our internal compass, pointing out when things go awry, or when we are on the right path. The reason that change elicits strong emotional reactions has a lot to do with human nature. Change propels us into the unknown, which is usually a place of uncertainty and insecurity. Fear of the unknown is one of the most common emotional reactions to change. Other common change-related fears are fear of failure, and fear of losing control.

> As leaders, it is our responsibility to guide our teams through change.

Beyond fear, change can also trigger emotions such as frustration, confusion, and even sadness or grief. Why grief, you might wonder? Well, change often involves letting go of the familiar, and the process of letting go can feel a lot like loss. However, change isn't all negative. It can also spark positive emotions, such as excitement, anticipation, and a sense of renewed energy. As leaders, we want to amplify those positive emotions.

Having identified the emotional landscape of change, how can we effectively manage people's reactions to it? The first step is empathy. Demonstrating empathy eases the emotional turbulence of change. It shows your team that you understand their feelings, and are committed to sharing the journey with them.

Next comes communication. Clear, transparent, and frequent communication can help dispel the uncertainty that often surrounds change. Sharing the "why" behind the change, explaining the benefits it will bring, and the plan to achieve it, can alleviate fear and build trust.

Lastly, help your team develop resilience. Encourage them to see change as an opportunity for growth rather than a threat. Equip them with the skills to navigate change effectively and provide them with the resources they need to succeed.

The emotional side of change is intertwined with the culture of an organization. A culture that is change-ready, where change is viewed as an integral part of growth, not as a disruption, has a solid foundation for a successful change initiative.

The ancient Chinese philosopher Lao Tzu said, "A leader is best when people barely know he exists ... when his work is done, his aim fulfilled, they will say: We did it ourselves." How do we build a change-ready environment, where our teams can say, "We did it ourselves!"?

Building a change-ready culture

Building a resilient, dynamic, and change-ready culture is a continuous process. Leadership guru John C. Maxwell said: "Change is inevitable. Growth is optional." Now is the time to choose growth, and build a foundation for it within our teams and organizations.

An organization is a community of individuals with unique skills, talents, and perspectives. Any change, no matter how small, has the capacity to have an impact on how the organization functions, and determine whether it thrives or withers. When positive change is implemented on a large scale, it can transform companies by unlocking new opportunities, inspiring innovation, and driving momentum. How do you create a change-ready culture in your organization?

1. **Lead by example** Any significant transformation starts at the top. As leaders, if we resist change, or are apprehensive about it, we can expect a similar response from our team members. Leaders must embrace change, champion its cause, and show enthusiasm, positivity, and resilience in the face of uncertainty. When your reaction to change is positive, your team members will be reassured, and motivated to accept change, too. Remember that as a leader, your behavior isn't just a drop in the ocean; it's the tide that shapes the shoreline.

2. **Develop a growth mindset** Carol Dweck, the psychologist who popularized the term "growth mindset", wrote: "In a growth mindset, challenges are exciting rather than threatening. So rather than thinking, 'Oh, I'm going to reveal my weaknesses', you say, 'Wow, here's a chance to grow'." Developing a growth mindset in your team means nurturing individual curiosity, innovation, and the courage to take risks. Failure should not be seen as a stumbling block, but as a springboard to resilience and innovation.

3. **Provide resources and support** Change can feel like standing at a closed door, not knowing what lies on the other side. As a leader, it is your role to equip your team with the tools, resources, and support they need to step into the unknown with confidence. Whether it's providing technical training, holding skills development workshops, mentoring, or giving individuals time to process and adapt to change, your support can make a difference in building a change-ready culture.

Guiding transformation

When it comes to implementing change, leaders guide the transformation process. Your job is to ensure that your team has a clear vision of how things will change in the future.

1. **Craft a comprehensive plan** Your first task as a change leader is to craft a detailed plan for transformation. The plan should state the vision foreseen by the change, outline the necessary steps to achieve this vision, indicate the roles and responsibilities of all team members, allocate resources, and set out strategies for managing potential risks.

2. **Facilitate transparent communication** A leader must convey to the entire team the reasons, objectives, and expectations of the change initiative. Addressing concerns, giving clear answers, and encouraging open dialogue will help your team feel engaged, and willing to commit to the process.

3. **Involve stakeholders** Actively engage with team members and other stakeholders (such as suppliers or customers). Let them know that you value their input and/or help to empower them in their new roles.

4. **Manage resistance** Resistance to change can stem from misunderstandings, fear of the unknown, or perceived loss. It is a natural response and, as a leader, it is your responsibility to empathically address concerns, provide reassurance, offer training, and/or refine the change plan based on the feedback received.

5. **Monitor progress and adjust strategy** Throughout the transformation process, you must regularly evaluate progress, measure results, gather feedback, and adjust strategies as needed.

6. **Celebrate milestones** Celebrations are a vital part of the change journey. They energize the team, strengthen commitment, and foster a culture of appreciation.

Giving structure to transformation

Among the many models for managing organizational transformation, ADKAR and Kotter's 8-Steps provide leaders with practical and methodical strategies for managing change. Both models highlight the importance of creating a compelling vision, communicating effectively, empowering individuals, and consolidating gains to make change stick. They help leaders steer their teams with clarity and confidence through the challenges and complexities of change.

The ADKAR model

This robust, practical model was developed in the 1990s by Jeff Hiatt, the founder of the change management firm Prosci. Its simplicity and effectiveness make it perennially popular among change leaders. By following five building blocks, or outcomes, you can guide your team through a transformation process, ensuring a successful outcome for your change initiative.

1. **Awareness** Understand the need for change. As a leader, it is your responsibility to explain why change is necessary, and what could happen if it is not implemented.

    Application Communicate regularly with your team, conveying up-to-date information and sharing success stories. Address any questions or concerns. If necessary, conduct one-on-one discussions to clarify details and facilitate their understanding of the process.

2. **Desire** Create a positive attitude towards change. Leaders must foster a collective desire to support and participate in any change initiatives.

    Application Where possible, involve team members in the change process. Address any concerns, and highlight the benefits of change for them personally, as well as for the organization. Appoint "change champions" who will support the initiative and encourage others to do the same.

205

3. **Knowledge** The information (data), skills, and/or training that teams need to make the change happen.

    Application Implement a training plan to equip your team with any practical skills or knowledge they lack. Make use of in-person workshops, e-learning modules, and on-the-job training. Additionally, provide resources for self-learning and encourage knowledge-sharing among team members.

4. **Ability** Turn knowledge into action. This is the practical application of what team members have learned.

    Application Provide opportunities for individuals to apply their new skills and knowledge. Offer constructive feedback, and celebrate successes. Role-playing and simulations may help employees practice new behaviors in a safe environment.

5. **Reinforcement** The process of embedding new behaviors or values into the organization's culture.

    Application Use performance metrics and regular check-ins to ensure that new behaviors are being practiced. Recognize and reward individuals and teams who successfully integrate change into their work. Seek continuous feedback and make any necessary adjustments to the change plan.

Kotter's 8 Steps for Leading Change

In his book, *Leading Change*, John P. Kotter introduced "8 Steps for Leading Change", which encourages leaders to approach organizational change in a systematic and structured manner. Recognizing the complexity of change, Kotter's model utilizes a step-by-step process to ensure that transformation will be effectively communicated, executed and sustained.

1. **Create a sense of urgency** Ensure that everyone understands why change is necessary, and why it is important right now. Clearly articulate the reasons for the change, the risks of maintaining the status quo, and the benefits of successful change. Use data, testimonials, and/or realistic scenarios to inspire your team.

2. **Form a powerful coalition** Gather a group of people who can drive the change. Identify key influencers; those with leadership skills, authority, expertise, and strong network connections. Involve them early in the process, and equip them with the resources to help lead the change.

3. **Develop a vision and strategy** A vision should be simple, vivid, and engaging. It outlines the state of the organization and provides a picture of the future that everyone can understand and rally around. A strategic plan sets out the steps needed to achieve this vision.

4. **Communicate the vision** Once the vision and strategy are in place, tell people about them via meetings, newsletters, intranet, and/or emails. Tailor your message for different audiences, but always ensure the message includes why the change is necessary.

5. **Empower broad-based action** Encourage individuals to contribute innovative ideas or solutions by removing barriers, such as unnecessary rules or bureaucracy. Provide resources and training to help people make the required changes.

6. **Celebrate short-term wins** Acknowledging short-term wins helps build momentum and validate the change effort. Easily achievable goals can act as early indicators of success, so celebrate all wins and recognize those who helped achieve them.

7. **Consolidate gains to produce more change** Don't declare victory too early; rather use the momentum you've achieved to promote further change. Use early successes as leverage to tackle bigger and more complex change elements. Strive for continuous improvement, and adjust the change process, based on feedback and lessons learned.

8. **Anchor new approaches in the culture** Make change a permanent part of the organizational culture by ensuring that new behaviors, processes, and practices are upheld. Anchor the changes by updating job descriptions, performance measures, and other formal mechanisms. Over time, reinforce the importance of the transformation through success stories and recognition.

STORY IN PRACTICE

Driving change

Over three decades, QuickServe Logistics had grown from a one-man operation to a mid-sized logistics business. Now, despite its reputation for efficiency and reliability, QuickServe was struggling. Thomas Dunbar, the founder, was ready to retire, and neither of his sons had expressed any interest in taking over. Dunbar believed his management team was still doing a good job, but rapid advances in technology required a different approach. It was time to bring in someone who could lead the company into a new era.

Hiroshi Tanaka was the man for the job. An individual possessing a remarkable degree of resilience and a high adaptability quotient (AQ), he had experience in managing organizational transformation, but this task was bigger than any he had tackled before. His role was not to just incorporate new technology, it was about persuading individuals to abandon entrenched habits and embrace new ways of doing things. Wanting the best for his business, Dunbar made it clear that Tanaka had the option of retaining the current leadership team, or replacing them.

Hiroshi felt that Kotter's "8-steps" offered a roadmap for the transformation he intended. But before proceeding, he wanted to address the emotions that come with any major change. Uncertainty, fearfulness, doubt, resistance, even anger, are common reactions to the loss of familiar processes and work habits. Hiroshi met one-on-one with each member of the leadership team. Anticipating that they might be reluctant to voice any fears or concerns, his true purpose was to observe their body language and other non-verbal indicators.

In meetings with older employees, he promised to honor the company's legacy while equipping it for the future. To the younger executives, he expressed the hope that they would embrace the challenge of transforming the tradition-bound company into a major player in the logistics industry.

In a company-wide meeting, Hiroshi pledged that open communication would be a hallmark of his leadership, and this would begin immediately. His presentation on trends in the logistics industry focused on advances in technology. Turning to the financials, he stressed that the company was still profitable, and pointed to signs of improvement. After giving feedback from current and past customers, he opened the floor to discussion.

For the next hour, Hiroshi answered questions from employees who wanted to know more about the proposed changes, the impact new technology would have on existing jobs, the cost implications of large-scale transformation, and when it was going to take place. By the time the meeting ended, Hiroshi believed he had accomplished the first of Kotter's eight steps: "Create a sense of urgency". He felt that his leadership team understood how important it was for the company to align with the rest of the logistics industry.

That meeting laid the foundation for Kotter's second step "Form a coalition to drive change". Despite some changes to the management team, it wasn't long before the third step "Develop a vision and strategy" resulted in a statement that resonated with everyone: Create a customer-centric, technology-driven logistics company that is ahead of the curve.

Over the coming months, Kotter's framework continued to guide the change process. Maintaining his promise of open communications, Hiroshi kept his team informed every step of the way. He ensured that project milestones were celebrated, and setbacks were viewed as opportunities for growth. A culture of learning enabled employees to acquire new skills, while Hiroshi's empathic approach and resilient spirit helped the team persevere through the most challenging aspects of transformation.

After months of intense effort, the once-traditional company was now at the forefront of technology-driven logistics solutions. As performance standards improved and targets were met, QuickServe gained greater profitability, and its reputation was restored.

However, Hiroshi considered his biggest achievement to be the transformation of his team. Having conquered the challenge, they were ready to lead the business with confidence and competence.

Hiroshi Tanaka's story is a testament to the power of adaptive leadership. Leading change goes beyond implementing new processes. It is about building a resilient and adaptable culture. To do that, you need to understand how to guide people in a new direction, and equip them with the tools to tackle challenges and overcome obstacles. Effective change management is not just about surviving the storm; it is about learning to dance in the rain.

SELF-REFLECTION PIT STOP

Scan the QR code or visit drtomdreyer.com/tools to download your e-toolkit.

Dealing with change and uncertainty

1. **Evaluate your resilience** Reflect on a challenge that you overcame. How did you handle it? How did you bounce back? Write down your strengths, and areas for improvement. Consider how you could use these strengths to bolster your resilience.

2. **Assess your adaptability** Consider a recent situation where you had to adapt quickly. Did you manage to do so effectively? What strategies did you use to adjust to the new situation? Identify areas where you could enhance your adaptability.

3. **Reflect on leading change** Think about a time when you led your team through a significant change. What strategies did you use? Were they effective? Reflect on what worked well and what didn't. Write down any improvements you could make in the future.

4. **Consider change-readiness** Assess your team's readiness for change. Do they understand the need for change, and are they equipped to handle it? Are there steps you could take to build a more change-ready culture within your team?

5. **Assess your adaptability quotient** Reflect on how you've managed change and uncertainty in the past. How quickly were you able to adjust your strategy or approach to meet new demands or circumstances? How might you improve your AQ?

6. **Set SMART goals** Identify key development areas, and set SMART goals for each area. For example: "Over the next four months, I will demonstrate my change management skills by conducting two workshops on change strategies. I will measure the effectiveness of the

workshops through post-event surveys that aim for at least 80% positive feedback." Outline the steps you will take to achieve these goals, the resources you'll need, and a timeline. Remember, self-improvement is a continuous journey.

Use this self-reflection pit stop as a checkpoint. Revisit your SMART goals and track your progress regularly. Acknowledge the progress you make. Continuously re-evaluate and reset your goals as you continue to grow as a resilient and adaptable leader.

Endnotes

1   Zheng, Y., Wu, T., Xu, J., Zhou, X., Yang, J., Liu, Y., ... & Yang, X. (2023). A multi-domain lifestyle intervention improves brain health and cognition in middle-aged adults: a randomized controlled trial. *Nature Neuroscience*, 26(10), 1405-1416.

2   Ding, X., Wu, X., Xu, J., Xu, Z., Yang, X., Liu, Y., ... & Yang, X. (2023). Effects of meditation on brain structure and function in major depressive disorder: A randomized controlled trial. *JAMA Psychiatry*, 80(9), 900-910.

3   Düzel, E., Bunzeck, N., Guitart-Masip, M., & Düzel, S. (2010). Novelty-related motivation of anticipation and exploration by dopamine (NOMAD): Implications for healthy aging. *Neuroscience & Biobehavioral Reviews*, 34(5), 660-669. https://doi.org/10.1016/j.neubiorev.2009.08.006

4   Davidson, R. J., & McEwen, B. S. (2012). Social influences on neuroplasticity: Stress and interventions to promote well-being. *Nature Neuroscience*, 15(5), 689-695. https://doi.org/10.1038/nn.3093

5   Gruber, M. J., Gelman, B. D., & Ranganath, C. (2014). States of curiosity modulate hippocampus-dependent learning via the dopaminergic circuit. *Neuron*, 84(2), 486-496. https://doi.org/10.1016/j.neuron.2014.08.060

6   Goleman, D. (1995). *Emotional intelligence*. Bantam Books.

STAR
1
⭐
**GROWING YOUR LEADERSHIP
SELF-AWARENESS**

STAR
2
⭐
DISCOVERING YOUR LEADERSHIP STYLE

STAR
3
⭐
UNDERSTANDING YOUR TEAM

STAR
4
⭐
BUILDING TRUST

STAR
5
⭐
DEVELOPING HIGH-PERFORMANCE TEAMS

STAR
6
⭐
THE POWER OF EI AND NLP

STAR
7
⭐
MASTERING COMMUNICATION

STAR
8
⭐
**RESILIENCE, ADAPTABILITY AND
TRANSFORMATION**

STAR
9
⭐
LEADING IN THE DIGITAL AGE

STAR
10
⭐
TALENT DEVELOPMENT

GOLDEN STAR

LEADING IN THE DIGITAL AGE

Digital transformation is an organizational change that integrates technology into every area of a business to fundamentally alter how it operates. It entails reinventing or replacing existing processes or systems with digitized, automated, cloud-based, and/or AI-driven solutions. As advances in technology remodel the corporate landscape, leaders must learn to manage remote teams, foster innovation, and harness the power of AI. They need to promote a culture of agility, openness, innovation, and customer-centricity. This Golden Star will help you develop the essential skills to lead a team in the digital age, ensuring you won't just survive, but thrive.

Meeting the challenge of digital transformation

Digital technology is integral to every facet of an organization. When done at a company-wide level, digital transformation isn't simply about swapping old tech for new; it frequently requires a complete overhaul of the entire business, including its operational models and cultural paradigms. Leading an organization through large-scale changes in technology requires a robust understanding of the impacts of digital disruption. Emerging technologies, such as artificial intelligence (AI), data analytics, cloud computing, automation, and more, don't merely change how we work; they revolutionize the essence of work itself.

As leaders, our mission is to create an environment that promotes continuous learning. We must encourage individuals to acquire new skills and competencies that equip them for work in an ever-evolving digital age. When change is the only constant, flexibility becomes a marketable asset.

Traditional leadership models, built on predictability and stability, will have less relevance in an era of continual, rapid change. To overcome this, we must cultivate agility within our teams, enabling them to swiftly adapt to change, while also encouraging risk-taking, and framing setbacks as opportunities for learning and innovation.

> Traditional leadership models, built on predictability and stability, will have less and less relevance in an era of continual, rapid change.

Transparency and communication are the key to managing digital transformation. We have already established that change can lead to resistance. Leaders need to articulate the reasons behind digital transformation, the advantages it will bring, and the steps required to accomplish it. Keeping teams informed, addressing hurdles candidly, and celebrating milestones, will build trust and boost morale, helping to develop a cohesive team.

> The first step in any transformation is to embrace change yourself.

The first step in any transformation is to embrace change yourself. As John C Maxwell puts it, "A leader is one who knows the way, goes the way, and shows the way." Your role as a leader is to foster a culture that willingly accepts change, and embraces it as an opportunity to learn and grow. Start with a clear understanding of how digital transformation aligns with the organization's strategic vision, and what this means for your team. You can't motivate other people unless you understand what you are asking them to do, so take advantage of every opportunity to familiarize yourself with the relevant technology.

Keep your team informed about the intended changes, explaining why they are necessary and the impact each change will have on their roles or functions. Cultivate a growth mindset and persuade individuals to see change as a learning opportunity. Encourage risk-taking, and remind them that setbacks are not failures, but stepping stones to innovation.

Remember, technology may provide the tools, but people are the operators. Equip your team with the skills they need to implement new technology. Invest in training and development programs that will upskill individuals appropriately. Promote a culture of self-learning, and encourage team members to take ownership of their personal development.

The implications of remote work

It seems as if the modern workspace has shrunk to fit our digital screens. The rise of remote work has reimagined the traditional concept of a team. Now, more often than not, teams are virtual, dispersed, and culturally diverse.

But while this offers exciting opportunities, it also presents challenges that leaders must navigate.

Neuroscience tells us that humans are wired for social connection and emotional engagement. When these are missing, as they often are in virtual environments, the challenge is to create bonds that inspire commitment.[1] The days when a team implied a collective of individuals working shoulder-to-shoulder in a single location are behind us. Nowadays, teams may consist of individuals spread across various time zones, operating from private dwellings, or shared workspaces. Diverse virtual teams have the potential to fuse a broad range of thoughts, ideas, and skill sets in ways that traditional teams simply can't match. However, leading a virtual team requires a refined leadership strategy, one backed by the cognitive insights that neuroscience provides.

> Diverse virtual teams have the potential to fuse a broad range of thoughts, ideas, and skill sets in ways that traditional teams simply can't match.

Effective communication is an important part of leading remote teams. Neuroscientific studies highlight the role of mirror neurons, a type of brain cell that responds equally when we perform an action or witness someone else performing the same action. Mirror neurons enable us to understand and mimic emotional states which, in turn, promote empathy and non-verbal communication.

In face-to-face interactions, mirror neurons contribute to our ability to intuit and resonate with others' feelings and intentions, which are conveyed though visual cues and body language.[2] When we communicate remotely, however, a lack of visual cues can diminish the effectiveness of our mirror neuron system, leading to a reduction in the emotional connections and/or level of understanding that would be natural in person-to-person interactions. As a result, messages can be more easily misinterpreted, resulting in confusion and miscommunication.

Communicating remotely can also impact on the richness of the inter-action. A lack of non-verbal cues, such as facial expressions and tone of voice, can strip down the emotional context of a message. This is particularly challenging for leaders who rely on non-verbal cues to gauge team morale and provide appropriate support.

To mitigate this, leaders must adopt communication strategies that compensate for the lack of physical presence. This includes being more explicit in verbal and written communication, using video calls and meetings to add a visual component to interactions, and fostering an environment that encourages open and frequent communication.

As a leader, it is your responsibility to ensure that all team members are aligned. In a remote context, over-communication is preferable to under-communication, so maintain frequent check-ins with team members to help maintain open communication channels.

When it comes to building successful remote teams, trust is a vital factor. The brain's oxytocin system, which underpins feelings of trust and social bonding, is generally less active during virtual interactions than it is in face-to-face situations. In a remote-work environment, leaders must trust their team members to execute their roles proficiently. Promoting a culture where results take precedence over hours logged allows you to shift from clock-watching to performance monitoring.

To cultivate a sense of community and shared purpose in a remote setup, introduce virtual team-building activities, collaborative online tools, and digital social spaces in the form of chat rooms and informal online get-togethers.

Despite challenges, the benefits of remote work are bountiful. In the corporate world, access to a global talent pool can be a game-changer. On a smaller scale, the benefits for employees, such as flexible hours and reduced commuting, may be as valuable. Neuroscience research confirms that, for individuals, a flexible work environment can decrease stress which, in turn, leads to improved mental health and increased productivity.[3] As a leader, your role is to maximize the benefits of remote work while minimizing the risks.

> Promoting a culture where results take precedence over hours logged allows you to shift from clock-watching to performance monitoring.

The confluence of AI and leadership: The future of work

Artificial intelligence (AI) is a phenomenon that stands out in its potential to revolutionize the workplace. Although it can be "disruptive", the AI revolution gives leaders an unprecedented opportunity to rethink traditional processes, and redefine the way teams work. AI is a tangible tool that leaders can leverage to drive efficiency, innovation, and growth.

AI is transforming business on every level. In addition to automating mundane tasks, and personalizing customer interactions, it has the capacity to perform tasks that require cognitive functions, such as problem-solving, perception, language-understanding, and decision-making. Used correctly, it can free up time, allowing leaders and employees to focus on strategic or creative tasks that add value. For instance, the time-consuming process of data analysis can be done quickly and accurately with AI, allowing leaders to make informed decisions more rapidly.

Integrating AI into an organization will require adaptation and change. Leaders should be ready to implement whatever upskilling or reskilling projects may be required to prepare their teams for the opportunities of an AI-driven future.

While AI offers exciting prospects, it also raises ethical considerations. As leaders, how do we ensure the responsible use of AI? Can we mitigate bias? How do we strike a balance between AI and human leadership? The journey towards a technologically advanced future requires careful thought and deliberate action.

The ethics of AI

Introducing AI into a business requires understanding the ethical implications. AI learns from data. Therefore, if data is biased (skewed), AI will internalize the bias and propagate it, leading to unfair and/or potentially harmful outcomes. Reputable AI systems are trained on representative (unbiased) data, continuously monitored for signs of bias or discrimination, and corrected as necessary.

Some AI algorithms, especially deep-learning models, are referred to as "black boxes" due to their complexity and the difficulty in understanding how they make decisions. Good systems strive for algorithmic transparency in order to build trust among their users.

There is widespread concern about the impact of AI on jobs and employment. Because AI enhances productivity and efficiency, it has the potential to automate certain roles, which can lead to job losses. Good leaders should use AI to augment human capabilities, not replace them entirely, and ensure that robust upskilling and reskilling programs are in place.

Data privacy is another concern. AI systems rely on large amounts of data, some of it sensitive or personal. Data must be collected, stored, and used responsibly, in line with national and international data protection laws, and with respect for individual privacy rights.

Adopting AI should be about balancing technological advancement with ethical considerations. The aim is to leverage AI to achieve business objectives, while upholding the values and principles that define us as human beings.

Skills for the future: Developing digital leadership competencies

Leadership in the digital age is not just about understanding technology. It is about fostering a culture of adaptability and continuous learning. Leaders must recognize the need for new competencies, even if it requires redefining their capabilities. While traditional leadership skills are still relevant, they may no longer be sufficient. Today's leaders need skills that will allow them to function and thrive in a technologically advanced workplace. Leadership competencies for a digital future include:

1. **Digital literacy** Understand the potential, as well as the implications, of using digital tools and technologies to shape your industry. You don't have to become a tech expert, but try to have a working knowledge of the applicable technological landscape.
2. **Data-driven decision-making** The ability to interpret and apply data is crucial. But before you can fully use data to guide your leadership strategy, measure performance, or make informed decisions, you need a basic understanding of data analytics and its impact on business operations and strategy.

3. **Agility and adaptability** In a rapidly evolving digital landscape, an agile and adaptable mindset makes it easier to respond swiftly to any changes or disruptions.

4. **Innovation and creativity** To stay competitive, you need to build a culture of innovation and creativity. Be open to new ideas, encourage risk-taking, and think of setbacks as steps towards success.

5. **Cybersecurity awareness** Understand the risks associated with accessing and storing large amounts of data. Cybersecurity means maintaining the security and integrity of organizational and customer data at all times.

6. **Digital ethics** The ethical implications of digital technologies are profound. Be equipped to make decisions that balance technological advancement with moral considerations.

7. **Digital communication** Managing remote workers and virtual teams requires leaders to master communication tools and techniques that facilitate effective online communication and collaboration.

8. **Continuous learning mindset** Continuously update your skills and knowledge to keep up with the pace of change.

Leveraging technology to lead

Digital tools enable leaders to interact remotely with their teams, streamline day-to-day operations and processes, and harness the collective intelligence of their employees.

1. **Communication platforms** Tools such as Microsoft Teams, Zoom, Google Meet, Slack, and many more, have changed the way we communicate and collaborate. These platforms offer real-time communication via voice and/or video calls, virtual team meetings, video conferencing, file sharing, and more. They are ideal for managing remote or dispersed teams, so leaders must be adept at using them effectively to maintain clear lines of communication and build rapport and trust with their team members.

2. **Project management tools** Apps such as Asana, Trello, and Jira can be used to track projects, assign tasks, monitor progress, and ensure

accountability. They promote transparency and enable teams to collaborate efficiently, no matter where they are located.

3. **Data analysis tools** Programs and apps such as Excel, Tableau, and Google Analytics can both analyze and visualize data, making it easier to make informed decisions, measure performance, and gain insights.

4. **Online education** To stay on top of the latest trends and develop new skills, sign up for online education and development courses. Coursera for Business, Udemy for Business, and LinkedIn Learning are some of the many offerings available.

5. **Learning management systems (LMS)** Platforms such as Moodle, Blackboard, Canvas, SAP SuccessFactors, and TalentLMS offer robust solutions for education and training. These systems enable leaders to develop, distribute, and oversee training content and courses specifically designed for their teams' developmental needs. With functionalities such as progress tracking, performance assessments, and a centralized repository for educational materials, learning management systems are invaluable for training new team members, upskilling current staff, and ensuring uniform training across the organization.

6. **Social media platforms** Sites such as LinkedIn, X (formerly Twitter), Facebook, and Yammer (Viva Engage) are suitable for informal communications, such as celebrating team achievements, or sharing details about the launch of a new product. Bear in mind, though, that not everyone uses social media as a source of information. Consider it an add-on, not a primary means of communicating.

7. **Cybersecurity tools** Leaders need to understand the implications of digital threats, and utilize cybersecurity tools to protect sensitive information. This could include ensuring that everyone uses a virtual private network (VPN) for secure connections, and complies with protocols for password management and protecting data.

8. **AI-powered tools** These analyze vast amounts of complex data to solve problems, provide outcomes, and predict trends. Everyday examples include chatbots, which use natural language processing to respond to customer enquiries; online grocery shopping, which uses your previous orders to suggest items to include in your basket; and notifying customers of new products or special offers that might interest

them. The benefits for businesses include improved decision-making, automating repetitive tasks, and personalizing customer experiences.

Take time to learn how to use digital tools effectively. Don't expect results overnight. Start with a clear goal in mind, because once you know what you want to achieve, it will be easier to identify the right tools for the job. This is a fast-changing field, so do research to find solutions that match your needs. As a leader, don't try to implement too many digital tools at once. Start with one or two tools, and see how they work for your team. To remain adaptable, be open to investigating new tools as they emerge.

Digital leaders are innovative leaders

Technology is not an end in itself, but a means to work more effectively and creatively. Leaders need to be conscious of the shifting requirements of employees and clients. They encourage their teams to remain curious, and be open to learning new things.

An innovative leader embodies a growth mindset, and recognizes that there is always room for new skills and knowledge. They commit to lifelong learning, and keep up with advances in technology. Leaders who embrace continuous learning are more likely to foster a culture of growth and development because they lead by example, motivating their team members to become lifelong learners themselves.

By promoting adaptability, leaders help their teams develop resilience in the face of change and uncertainty. This involves nurturing an environment where change is seen as an opportunity for growth. Adaptability requires leaders to be flexible in their strategies and willing to pivot when circumstances demand it.

Innovative leaders recognize that great ideas can come from unexpected sources. They encourage collaboration, diversity of thought, and open communication, and ensure every team member feels valued and empowered to contribute. This builds a sense of collective ownership, and commitment to the company's success.

Innovation is not just about generating new ideas, but also executing them effectively. To do this, you need to balance creativity with critical analysis. Ensure new ideas are both viable, and align with the company's strategic objectives. Be willing to take calculated risks and learn from setbacks, viewing them as valuable learning opportunities.

STORY IN PRACTICE

Transforming Queen Grocery

For over fifty years, the family-owned Queen Grocery operated several small stores across the borough of Queens in New York City. The chain was founded in 1972 by Morris Townsend, a hard-working, modest man who worked the cash register until well into his 70s, even though he had a controlling share in the business. The day-to-day operations were in the hands of his son and daughter-in-law, so for Morris, work was an excuse to chat with long-time customers and employees. After Townsend's death, the family sold the business to a company that managed similar retail operations throughout the eastern seaboard. They hired an industry veteran, Kenny Mancini, to revitalize the chain.

Mancini recognized that significant work lay ahead. In recent years, the Townsend family had ignored the changing demographics that transformed the borough into vibrant, ethnically diverse neighborhoods. The stores had become drab and outdated, and lacked industry-standard technology, such as self-checkout scanners. In addition to revamping the interiors and exteriors, Mancini recognized the need to implement the appropriate technology to make Queen Grocery stores appealing for busy suburbanites seeking good service, and a wide range of products at competitive prices.

A successful digital transformation would require acceptance by both staff and customers. As a business, Queen Grocery had not been profitable for some time, but the stores had a loyal following, and Mancini believed that retaining a sense of community needed to be a factor in returning the chain to profitability.

During his store visits, Mancini talked to customers and employees, asking what they liked or didn't like, and whether the products on offer met the needs of the diverse communities in which they were located. He also asked store managers and back-office staff whether they had all the tools they needed to do their jobs.

As a digital transformation plan formed in his mind, he kept everyone informed. He investigated how technology could improve various departments, and whether the managers anticipated acceptance or resistance from suppliers, staff, and/or customers. He had discussions with HR over the possible termination of older and long-serving employees who might struggle to adapt to new technology, and replacing them with younger "digital natives" drawn from the surrounding neighborhoods.

Mancini's digital transformation plan focused on the creation of a loyalty app, which offered a range of features, from special offers, promotional coupons and weekly menus to customized shopping lists based on dietary preferences. The app supported online shopping, with options for delivery or curbside pickup. Customers eagerly signed up, and online shopping soon became a profitable part of the business.

Since loyalty card purchases can yield personal information based on a shopper's habits and choices, even to approximating the number and/or ages of people in a household, Mancini remained alert to the ethical implications of AI. Protecting personal data required the company to invest in cybersecurity, but having access to data on shopping habits enabled the marketing department to create targeted promotions ahead of significant cultural celebrations, such as Chinese New Year, Diwali, and Halloween. And, of course, customers had the option to opt out if they chose.

Back-office functions, such as inventory management, point-of-sale pricing, staffing schedules, and quarterly sales projections, were revitalized by the implementation of data analytics software. By improving warehousing and distribution, for example, the system optimized centralized buying, and the resulting cost savings could be passed on to the customer.

Mancini modeled his approach on what he had learned from other leaders. He read articles and took online courses on implementing digital change in the retail industry, and encouraged his managers to do the same. Recognizing that digital tools offered not just operational benefits, he introduced project management tools to facilitate communication between stores. Thanks to his belief in learning through experience, he encouraged his team to take calculated risks, learn from failures, and continually seek better ways of doing things.

It wasn't long before Mancini's efforts yielded results. With more customers coming through the doors, sales increased and the balance sheet turned from red to black. Digital technology brought improvements in efficiency, but the real bonus was the level of engagement by customers and staff, all of whom welcomed the revitalization of this once-fading chain.

The story of Kenny Mancini and Queen Grocery is one of bold leadership in the midst of a digital revolution. It highlights the importance of embracing change, maintaining ethical integrity, and fostering a culture of innovation, adaptation and learning.

SELF-REFLECTION PIT STOP

Scan the QR code or visit drtomdreyer.com/tools to download your e-toolkit.

Adopting digital transformation

1. **Map the digital landscape** Consider the ways in which large-scale digital transformation within the company might have an impact on, or benefit, your team.

2. **Tech as a leadership aid** Which technological tools do you currently use? Are there gaps that new tools could fill? Explore new platforms that could enhance your ability to lead your team through digital change.

3. **Future-proof your skills** Do you have confidence in your digital competencies, or is there room for improvement? (Remember, this is not limited to technical skills; it also applies to soft skills like adaptability, resilience, and digital communications.)

4. **Embrace remote work** Do you have the necessary technical know-how to facilitate remote communication and online collaboration within your team? If not, can you identify the required training or upskilling opportunities for you and your team members?

5. **AI and leadership intersection** How do you foresee AI influencing your leadership style in the future? What are the risks and/or opportunities for you, personally?

6. **Ethics in the AI era** How will you ensure that your team upholds the ethical considerations of AI in their day-to-day roles?

7. **The innovation imperative** How will you leverage technological innovation within your team? What can you can do to encourage individuals to adopt new tech options?

8. **Set SMART goals** Identify opportunities for digital innovation, or the introduction of new technology. For example: "Over the next six months, I will hold a virtual 'Innovation Hour' each month, during which team members can share their ideas on how technology might benefit our projects. The goal is to implement at least one new idea into our workflow each quarter."

As we move into our next Golden Star, we'll delve into a fundamental leadership responsibility: developing others. Great leaders do not just lead; they inspire, empower, and cultivate the leaders of tomorrow. Golden Star 10 explores the interface between leadership and talent development.

Endnotes

1   Meyer, M. L., & Lieberman, M. D. (2018). Why social pain can live on: Different neural mechanisms are associated with reliving social and physical pain. *PLOS ONE*, 13(6), e0197333. https://doi.org/10.1371/journal.pone.0197333

2   Jiang, M., & Varnum, M. E. W. (2021). Cultural differences in the mirror neuron system response: A 3T fMRI study. *NeuroImage*, 224, 117433. https://doi.org/10.1016/j.neuroimage.2020.117433

3   Allen, T. D., Golden, T. D., & Shockley, K. M. (2015). How effective is telecommuting? Assessing the status of our scientific findings. *Psychological Science in the Public Interest*, 16(2), 40-68. https://doi.org/10.1177/1529100615593273

STAR 1 — GROWING YOUR LEADERSHIP SELF-AWARENESS

STAR 2 — DISCOVERING YOUR LEADERSHIP STYLE

STAR 3 — UNDERSTANDING YOUR TEAM

STAR 4 — BUILDING TRUST

STAR 5 — DEVELOPING HIGH-PERFORMANCE TEAMS

STAR 6 — THE POWER OF EI AND NLP

STAR 7 — MASTERING COMMUNICATION

STAR 8 — RESILIENCE, ADAPTABILITY AND TRANSFORMATION

STAR 9 — LEADING IN THE DIGITAL AGE

STAR 10 — TALENT DEVELOPMENT

GOLDEN STAR

10

TALENT
DEVELOPMENT

Today's leaders inspire, empower, and cultivate the leaders of tomorrow. In order to do this, you must first identify potential leaders, and then set out to nurture them. This Golden Star explores the role that leaders play in recognizing and developing talent. A "talent developer" is a leader who empowers others by improving their competence and skills. In this chapter, you will explore the various developer styles, and learn how to use the power of coaching to unlock potential in others. We'll also discover a new approach to one-on-one mentoring, the skill of delegation, and how to become a multiplier of capability and competence within your team.

Discover your developer style

Every leader possesses a unique way of developing talent in others. This instinctive "compass" is shaped by neural pathways in our brain, and influences how we guide others, and support their growth. Recognizing your personal developer style starts with acknowledging the complex cognitive processes that constantly take place in our brains. It is about equipping yourself with a range of mental tools, and knowing how to utilize them. In all likelihood, you will lean towards one style but, just as neuroplasticity allows our brain to adapt and change, effective leadership requires fluidity. Good leaders have the ability to adjust their approach based on the situation, the needs of the individual, and their own instincts.

Doctor Just as a medical doctor prescribes treatment, a coach who leans towards the doctor style will tend to diagnose situations, devise solutions, and provide specific instructions. While this prescriptive style can be valuable in situations that demand immediate action, it is important to let team members develop their own problem-solving skills. Leaders who adopt the Doctor style display brain patterns associated with decision-making and problem-solving. However, they need to adapt their instinctive decision-making mindset to incorporate empathy and flexibility.

Expert This style is characterized by the ability to sell knowledge, skills, or ideas. Expertise stems from a highly developed set of neural connections. As a leader, your proficiency might be invaluable to your team, but take care not to overshadow their individual learning processes. The brain learns most effectively through experience, so allowing team members to discover their own solutions will enrich them.

Coach By drawing on the brain's empathic and social circuits, coaches play a supportive role. Instead of presenting solutions, they encourage individuals to identify their strengths and opportunities, and seek their own solutions. Asking insightful questions triggers reflective thinking, which taps into the prefrontal cortex's decision-making functions. Supportive coaching builds resilience and stimulates personal growth, but achieving this requires time and mutual commitment. With patience, the gradual, reinforcing nature of learning generates a change in our brain.

Counselor In this nurturing role, counselors prioritize giving advice, guidance, and emotional support. They use active listening, understanding and empathy to foster trust, and create strong bonds with others. These bonds are enhanced by neurological impulses generated by the amygdala, the brain's emotional centre, and by the release of oxytocin, a bonding hormone. Counselors must remember to maintain professional boundaries in order to balance emotional support with individual accountability.

Coaching

Leaders are tasked with bringing out the best in others by unlocking their potential. Coaching develops future leaders by fostering personal and professional growth, and helps individuals to discover their strengths, overcome their challenges, and reach their goals.

Coaching is based on the principle of developing rather than directing. As a coach, your role isn't to provide solutions, it is to guide individuals towards finding their own answers. Coaching conversations are not intended to instruct, advise, or solve problems. They are about asking insightful questions, practicing active listening, and giving constructive feedback that will drive performance. The skills you have acquired in the other Golden Stars will contribute towards making you a better coach.

Thought-provoking questions require introspection and critical thinking, and prioritize self-discovery. To grow, we need to understand that we are not limited by our circumstances, only by our thinking, and that changing your mindset can open the door to limitless growth.

Think about the most impactful conversation you have ever had. It will probably be one where you felt heard, seen, and understood, or which made you think, reflect, and recognize something essential about yourself. A coaching conversation has the power to make us re-evaluate our beliefs, challenge our limits, and reveal our strengths.

Careful questioning helps individuals identify their mistakes, learn from them, and develop strategies to avoid repeating them in the future. As a leader, you may adopt different coaching styles at different times. For example, imagine that one of your team members was distressed because a project was not going as planned. As a mentor, you might adopt the doctor style, and tell them what to do in order to get back on track. In contrast, a coaching approach would ask open-ended questions such as "What do you think went wrong?" or "What can you learn from this?".

Stephen R. Covey said, "Most people do not listen with the intent to understand; they listen with the intent to reply." A good coach should always listen with empathy and understanding. When you genuinely listen to what someone is saying, and sense their underlying needs, your coaching conversations will become significantly more effective and impactful.

Coaching promotes ownership and accountability. Allowing individuals to come up with their own solutions makes them more invested in implementing them. When someone takes responsibility for their actions, they discover that instead of being a passive recipient of change, they become an active participant in their own development journey.

Coaching techniques

Many practical techniques are supported by neuroscience insights. Recent studies on decision-making and meditation highlight the neural mechanisms that underpin our coaching strategies.[1]

Ask open-ended questions Questions are the cornerstone of effective coaching. While closed-ended questions can generally only be answered with "yes" or "no", open-ended questions invite expansive thinking and/ or self-reflection. Asking, "What solution would you choose?" instead of "Do you think Option A will work?", allows the respondent to consider different possibilities.

Neuroscience insight: Open-ended questioning activates the prefrontal cortex, the area of the brain associated with complex thinking and planning. Cognitive flexibility and creative problem-solving allow individuals to explore a range of solutions.

Encourage reflective thinking Ask team members to reflect on their past experiences, actions, or decisions and how they might impact on their choices going forward. For example: "How did your previous experience inform your current approach?" or "Looking back, what could you have done differently?"

Neuroscience insight: Reflective thinking activates the part of the brain that is linked to self-referential thought processes. This helps individuals connect their past experiences with present actions, fostering deeper learning and self-awareness.

Practice active listening This goes beyond just *hearing* words; it involves processing what you hear, understanding it, and responding thoughtfully. When you create a space for someone to speak, and focus on what they are saying, they will feel heard and valued.

Neuroscience insight: When we actively listen, we engage mirror neurons in our brain, which are responsible for empathy and understanding, and connect us with the speaker's emotions and intentions. Neural mirroring fosters trust and rapport, which play an essential role in a coaching relationship.

Give constructive feedback This can be a powerful tool for personal growth, but make sure your feedback is helpful, not harmful. Adopting the sandwich technique, where criticism is nestled between positive comments, will ensure that feedback is perceived as both balanced and motivational.

Neuroscience insight: Positive feedback triggers the release of dopamine, a neurotransmitter associated with feelings of reward and satisfaction. Conversely, negative feedback can activate the amygdala, inducing a defensive response. Balancing constructive feedback with positive affirmation ensures that the brain remains receptive to the idea of change.

Empathic understanding Having empathy means considering how your team members feel, and being responsive to their emotions. It's about validating people's feelings and perspectives, and creating an environment of mutual respect.

Neuroscience insight: Practicing empathy stimulates the brain's limbic system, particularly the amygdala, which plays a role in emotional processing. Empathy helps leaders build deeper and more meaningful connections with their team members.

Role-playing and scenario-based exercises Integrating role-playing into coaching sessions lets team members test their responses to various scenarios. Being able to experiment in a safe space will enhance their problem-solving and decision-making skills.

Neuroscience insight: Role-playing stimulates creative thinking, promotes adaptability, and helps prepare team members for real-life situations.

Adopt a solution-focused approach Shifting the focus from dwelling on problems to seeking solutions encourages teams to consider their desired outcome and explore ways to achieve it.

Neuroscience insight: Actively seeking solutions leverages the phenomenon of neuroplasticity, the brain's ability to rewire itself. It helps team members reframe their thinking patterns, and move from a fixed mindset to a growth-oriented one.

Visualizing goals Encourage team members to visualize how they might achieve their goals. For example, they could picture the steps needed to accomplish a specific task, consider what they will do to overcome any challenges they encounter, and think about how they will feel when the goal is achieved.

Neuroscience insight: Visualization activates the same neural networks that we use for performing actual tasks. Mental rehearsal strengthens these neural pathways, making the envisioned actions or objectives more achievable in real life.

Positive recognition Acknowledge the achievements and progress of others. Recognition can be delivered one-on-one, in team meetings, or via written communications.

Neuroscience insight: Positive recognition stimulates the release of the neurotransmitter dopamine, which enhances feelings of pleasure and motivation. It reinforces desired behaviors, and contributes to a positive team environment.

Celebrate success Don't save celebrations for big wins. Celebrating even small victories and incremental gains by team members helps maintain motivation and momentum.

Neuroscience insight: Celebrating personal victories and/or team achievements triggers the brain's reward pathways, resulting in a sense of accomplishment that motivates further progress.

Applying the GROW model to coaching

Developed specifically for coaching, the GROW model (Goal, Reality, Options, Way Forward), utilizes the techniques of problem-solving, goal setting, and personal improvement, all of which are instrumental in unlocking individual potential.

The first step is to set SMART goals (Specific, Measurable, Achievable, Realistic, Time-bound), which can be used to direct a personal coaching conversation. As a leader-coach, you can help team members articulate their goals by asking open-ended questions such as, "What do you want to achieve?", "How will you measure success?" or "How did you determine the time frame for the project?".

The second step is to evaluate the current reality or situation. Identify any challenges or obstacles that might stand in the way of achieving the stated goals or objectives, and consider what resources you have to overcome them. As a coach, ask questions such as, "What have you tried so far?" or "What obstacles are holding you back?".

Next, consider all the options for reaching the goals. Encourage team members to think out of the box by asking questions like, "If you had unlimited resources, what would you do?".

The final step is to establish an action plan, or "way forward" to achieve the goals. As this must be realistic and achievable, with a degree of accountability, ask questions such as, "How do you plan to overcome any obstacles?" or "How will you monitor progress?".

Mentoring

Coaching fosters individual growth and unlocks potential in future leaders. Mentoring transfers organizational knowledge and experience from one generation to the next. It is a relationship-based developmental system where an experienced individual (the mentor) offers guidance, support, and wisdom to a less experienced person (the mentee). In leadership, mentoring is a potent tool for transferring knowledge and building organizational capacity, as well as for promoting career growth in others. Mentoring transcends the boundaries of a transactional relationship to create a relationship that is based on interpersonal connection, mutual growth, and shared understanding.

Benefits of mentoring

1. **Knowledge transfer** Emotional intelligence (EI) plays a huge role in effective mentoring. A mentor uses not only their technical skills and institutional knowledge, but also their own EI to guide their mentee. This results in a rich transfer of skills, wisdom, and tacit knowledge, which is not easily captured in any manual or process document.
2. **Career development** A mentor provides insights into the unwritten rules and conventions of an organization. In this way, they help the mentee navigate the often-complex terrain of professional growth and career development.

3. **Retention and engagement** Investing in employees, and making them feel valued, increases their level of job satisfaction and sense of commitment. This, in turn, contributes to better retention rates within an organization.

4. **Personal growth** Mentoring someone can enhance your own personal growth. The unique relationship that is built during the mentoring process allows for deep self-reflection and encourages mentors to step out of their comfort zones.

A neuroscience approach to effective mentoring

Effective mentoring requires deliberate practice and understanding. Here are five ways to enhance your mentoring approach, supported by insights from neuroscience:

1. **Build trust** At the heart of every mentoring relationship is trust. Neuroscience shows that trust involves the brain's limbic system, which is crucial for emotional processing.[2] As a mentor, it is essential to be dependable, and to maintain confidentiality. Aligning your actions with your words, and creating a safe space for open dialogue, develops trust between mentor and mentee.

2. **Engage in active listening** To truly understand your mentee's perspectives, you need to listen to what they have to say, and provide a safe space in which they can express themselves. Active listening activates the brain's mirror neurons, which play a role in boosting empathy and understanding.[3]

3. **Personalize your approach** Leadership guru Tony Robbins was renowned for his personal approach. You can emulate him by tailoring your mentoring style to each mentee's specific needs and aspirations. This resonates with neuroplasticity; the brain's ability to reorganize itself by forming new neural connections.[4] Recognizing a mentee's unique neural make-up and way of learning will help to make you a more effective mentor.

4. **Encourage independence** Exploring new opportunities, and taking risks fosters a growth mindset. This is neurologically linked to increased motivation, and the pursuit of challenges.[5] However, your aim must be to nurture your mentee's potential, not create a clone of yourself.

5. **Provide constructive feedback** Regular and balanced feedback is crucial for growth. Neuroscience suggests that receiving effective feedback activates areas of the brain associated with learning and self-reflection,[6] and helps mentees recognize their strengths, and discover areas for development.

The CASCADE mentoring model

The CASCADE mentoring model, which I developed, can be adapted to meet the unique needs of each mentee. Mentoring should not be a one-size-fits-all; it should be a flexible process that evolves with the mentee. Effective mentoring requires a considerable investment of both time and effort, but the benefits include enhanced performance, transfer of knowledge, and clear succession planning. Implementing the CASCADE model will make growth for your team a reality, not an option. By becoming a mentor, you are building a legacy of leadership within your organization.

The model is designed for regular evaluation. Working together, mentor and mentee will assess progress, redefine goals, and plan further coaching and/or development sessions, as required.

- **Connect and clarify** The first step is to connect. Establishing a relationship based on mutual trust and respect allows you to clarify personal goals as well as identify work roles and how they fit into the team's strategic plan. Connecting on a personal level requires an understanding of the mentee's aspirations, strengths, and potential areas for growth.

- **Assess the current status** Through a series of conversations, the mentor assesses the mentee's knowledge and competencies against the requirements of the job, and highlights any areas of weakness. The process should not be one-sided. Encourage your mentee to use self-assessment, as well as feedback from others, to establish their own status.

- **Set goals** Working together, set SMART goals that align with the mentee's career progression, as well as with both the team's objectives and objectives of the organization.
- **Coach with a purpose** Provide guidance and support as the mentee moves towards meeting their goals. Purposeful coaching requires active listening and giving constructive feedback. It allows the mentor to cultivate the mentee's capabilities, and encourage them to consider solutions, even if this pushes them beyond their comfort zone.
- **Advise on a plan** Use your experience and knowledge to tailor a personal development plan for your mentee. The plan should align with departmental and organizational strategies. Having an active plan will guide the mentee through any obstacles they encounter in their career.
- **Develop and implement strategies** Once you have a plan in place, encourage the mentee to acquire new skills, improve existing ones, and take on challenges that will lead to further growth and development.
- **Evaluate** Meet regularly with your mentee to provide feedback and review progress. Discuss what is working and what is not, and determine what needs to change. If necessary, adjust the action plan. Evaluation should also recognize the mentee's accomplishments and provide positive affirmation where applicable.

CASCADE MENTORING MODEL

C	**CONNECTION**	Establish a relationship based on trust and respect.
A	**ASSESS**	Assess skills, knowledge, and competencies.
S	**SET GOALS**	Together, define clear, achievable SMART goals.
C	**COACH**	Provide guidance, support, and challenges.
A	**ADVISE**	Guide through obstacles and navigate through their career.
D	**DEVELOP**	Focus on professional and personal development.
E	**EVALUATE**	Provide constructive feedback and recognition of accomplishments.

Delegation

Successful leaders know that delegation is a valuable tool for empowering others, as well as for their own personal development. Willingness to delegate is often seen as an indication of leadership potential. Cultivating this skill in others will expand the pool of talent that can step into leadership roles when the time is right.

Delegation is about trust. It requires having faith in people's abilities, and entrusting them with tasks that were once solely your responsibility. This benefits the leader, because it frees them to focus on strategic decisions and big-picture thinking, but it also greatly benefits the individual in whom trust has been placed.

From a neuroscience perspective, being trusted taps into the brain's reward system. Being given responsibility boosts morale and motivation, generating neurological reactions that stimulate the release of dopamine, the neurotransmitter that is linked to pleasure and which, in turn, amplifies the intrinsic rewards associated with task completion.

Effective delegation requires understanding individual team members' skills and competencies, so that you know which tasks to delegate to whom. It requires setting clear goals and realistic deadlines, giving appropriate feedback, and providing the necessary resources to succeed.

Use SMART goals to establish a clear framework and avoid confusion or miscommunication. Having realistic expectations engages the prefrontal cortex, the part of the brain involved in planning and decision-making, and helps develop a positive growth mindset.

Building future leaders: Identifying potential

"A leader is great, not because of his or her power, but because of his or her ability to empower others." John C. Maxwell

Successful leaders create more leaders, not more followers. One of the main responsibilities of leadership is to identify potential in others, and nurture them. This starts with a keen eye for talent and the ability to spot individuals who demonstrate not just competence and intelligence, but also resilience, adaptability, vision, and a knack for inspiring and influencing others. Once you have identified individuals with potential, you can:

- **Create a development program** Ongoing training or mentorship not only equips high-potential individuals with leadership skills, it familiarizes them with the organization's strategic objectives. A leadership development program should include challenging assignments that expand an individual's levels of competence.
- **Invest in one-on-one time** Spending quality time with potential leaders gives you insight into their attitudes, values and career aspirations. Formal coaching sessions provide opportunities to give guidance and impart your leadership philosophy. Informal get-togethers allow you to just chat.
- **Promote collaboration** Encourage potential leaders to work in cross-functional teams. This will broaden their organizational knowledge, and develop their collaborative and influencing skills.

Succession planning goes hand-in-hand with developing skills and competencies that may be required by the organization in the future. Developing new talent will ensure continuity when job roles are left vacant by retirement or an unforeseen departure. A well-structured succession plan not only minimizes operational disruption, it opens a clear path of progression for key individuals, which can be incredibly motivating. The first steps are to:

- **Identify potential successors** Start by identifying which roles are critical to your team's operations. Then, based on personal performance and potential, identify existing team members who could step into these roles in the future.
- **Provide development opportunities** Once potential successors are identified, provide opportunities for personal development and/or skills training, coaching and mentoring. Offer challenging assignments that will prepare them for a future role.
- **Update the plan** Be prepared for unanticipated changes by regularly reviewing and updating your succession plan.

Multipliers: Amplifying intelligence and capabilities

The compelling framework of "Multipliers and Diminishers" was brilliantly conceptualized by Liz Wiseman and Greg McKeown in their seminal work, *Multipliers: How the Best Leaders Make Everyone Smarter*. Multipliers are forward-thinking leaders who amplify the potential of their teams by creating an environment where individuals feel valued, as well as challenged and stretched. They understand that both collaborative decision-making, and delegating authority, have the positive effect of multiplying people's inherent capabilities and intelligence. This strengthens the entire team by increasing overall levels of engagement and output. Becoming a multiplier not only boosts productivity and team morale, it enhances both personal and professional growth for leaders and team members. The role of a multiplier is to:

- **Maximize talent** Multipliers identify individual strengths, and place team members in roles or projects that optimize these. This makes multipliers talent magnets, attracting gifted individuals who crave a work environment where their skills and abilities will be fully engaged and appreciated.
- **Encourage best thinking** By having an open-door policy, where everyone's ideas are welcome and valued, multipliers stimulate people to consider things carefully and deliver their best thinking. They ignite a collective intelligence, where the wisdom of the crowd is amplified.
- **Drive innovation** Multipliers are able to articulate challenges in a way that stretches team members. Innovative solutions arise when individuals are invigorated by unexpected challenges or unforeseen opportunities. Just remember to provide the necessary tools, resources, and support to allow individuals to perform at their best.
- **Promote debate** Actively involving team members in decision-making promotes a culture of open discussion and debate. Multipliers understand that the quality of decision-making improves when different viewpoints can be freely expressed. This approach helps foster a sense of investment in how decisions are made.

- **Instill accountability** Multipliers know that when people are delegated to take charge of a project, they become accountable for it, and they feel personally responsible for the outcome. This drives motivation, commitment, and accountability.

Practical steps to becoming a multiplier

1. **Redefine your leadership mindset** This starts with viewing your team members as inherently intelligent, and capable of delivering remarkable results. Believe in their potential, and be confident that they can function with minimum supervision.

2. **Harness the power of inquiry** Change your mindset from "I must have all the answers" to one that asks challenging questions. This will encourage people to think for themselves, explore different options, and come up with innovative solutions.

3. **Practice active listening** Make a concerted effort to reduce your talk time and increase your listen time. Active listening not only shows respect for your team members' ideas, it equips you with valuable insights that can guide your own leadership decisions.

4. **Cultivate a culture that learns from mistakes** Drive home the message that it is okay to make mistakes, or get things wrong, provided this serves as a learning experience. When you promote a sympathetic approach, people will be unafraid to take risks.

5. **Delegate and empower** Don't just assign tasks. Delegate the authority to make decisions about how those tasks are accomplished. This gives team members a sense of autonomy and ownership, and significantly boosts their motivation.

Diminishers

Multipliers have positive impacts, diminishers do the opposite. They dampen spirits, create anxiety, fail to share knowledge and resources, and can make people feel undervalued and incapable. Diminishers like to be in control, and believe they have all the answers. As a result, they frequently underutilize the skills of their team. Instead of multiplying collective energy, diminishers reduce it.

Recognizing progress and celebrating achievements

We all yearn to be recognized for the work we do. When leaders actively acknowledge team and/or individual progress and growth, it sends a potent message that our efforts are valued. Recognition doesn't always have to involve grand gestures; a simple "well done" can go a long way towards boosting employee morale.

A key aspect of recognition is celebrating progress, even if the job is not complete. Instead of waiting for final results, leaders should acknowledge interim milestones. This includes both individual efforts and quantifiable outcomes. Similarly, celebrating personal growth, not just progress made, reinforces a culture of continuous learning and improvement.

In practice, recognition could be anything from approving an innovative approach to solving a problem, to commending a team member for mastering a new skill, or applauding someone for stepping out of their comfort zone. Always connect your recognition to the specific behaviors you want to promote. By doing so, you not only validate the individual's effort, you also model these behaviors for the entire team.

STORY IN PRACTICE

Mentoring: A path to success

When entrepreneur Tony Montero purchased a small manufacturing company, he knew it was struggling financially, but he believed he had the skills to restore it to profitability. However, a year later, the business was still not where he wanted it to be. Yes, finances had improved, production was flowing smoothly and orders were being delivered on time. So where did the problem lie?

Tony sought advice from a trusted mentor. After providing a lengthy explanation, Tony waited to hear what his friend had to say. The words were not what he expected. "Tony," he said, "You've told me all about your strategic planning, operating efficiency, equipment upgrades, and implementation of the latest technology, but nothing about your people. Do you even know how your leaders are performing? Can you tell me how engaged and motivated your employees are?"

As he thought about his mentor's words, Tony realized that, for the past year, his attention had been on turning around the production side of the business. He had neglected the human aspect. He hoped it was not too late to invest in his leadership team.

Tony knew there was inevitably some measure of conflict among talented and experienced leaders, but now he wondered if conflicting approaches could be undermining his strategy. Tony was a natural planner. If people were the "problem", his instinct was to develop a plan to fix it. Believing he had the right people in place, he decided to implement a development plan to bring out the best in his leaders.

The first step was to really get to know his management team. A series of one-on-one meetings gave him insight into their leadership styles, which influenced not only how they related to each other, but how they managed their teams. For example, confident, "expert" leaders might be resentful if someone with an authoritative "doctor" style told them what to do. On the other hand, a "coaching" or "counseling" style worked for employees who needed support and guidance. Tony realized that not only did his leaders have to find a way to work together, he had to adapt his own leadership style in order to bring out the best in his executives.

Successful relationships are based on trust. As Tony built up the level of trust between himself and his leaders, he worked at establishing relationships based on each person's style. For some, this meant applying coaching techniques, for others, engaging in active listening, or giving honest, open feedback. But the relationships that resonated most with Tony were those that involved mentoring.

In the early years of his career, Tony had received guidance and support from an empathic mentor. Now, he hoped he could become a mentor himself. Through mentoring, he hoped to create a support network that would provide the personal guidance and knowledge-sharing that was missing in the company.

Tony chose the CASCADE mentoring model as the best tool to mentor his leaders, and enable them to mentor their own team members. Following the steps outlined in the model. he began by connecting with his team leaders on a personal level, to clarify their roles and responsibilities. One-on-one conversations revealed their current competencies, and identified any limitations, which were then addressed through counseling sessions. The next step was to set SMART goals that aligned with each individual's personal development goals, as well as their team's objectives.

Coaching helped the leaders prepare to mentor their own team members. Workshops and training sessions covered topics such as active listening, constructive feedback, and delegation.

The team leaders now identified their mentees and developed plans to meet their needs, ensuring they aligned with the organizational goals. With the plans in place, mentors worked with their mentees to implement strategies for growth, ranging from one-on-one conversations and job shadowing to attending workshops or courses.

The final step was evaluation. Tony met quarterly with his leaders to review progress and recognize their accomplishments. He adjusted their personal development plans if necessary, and encouraged them to keep learning. Each mentor also met regularly with their own mentees. Through this diligent implementation of the CASCADE model, mentorship became a significant factor in the company's return to profitability.

As the leaders became multipliers of talent, they became catalysts for corporate growth and development. With every employee contributing to their fullest potential, business boomed. The once-failing company was back on the road to success. There were still occasional conflicts and setbacks, but the prevailing sentiment was one of collaboration, and a belief that the company's success depended on the success of everyone in it. Tony's strategy had paid off. By developing his leaders, he proved that, in business, success is as much about people as it is about processes.

SELF-REFLECTION PIT STOP

Scan the QR code or visit drtomdreyer.com/tools to download your e-toolkit.

Embracing the learner within

Use this self-reflection pit stop to evaluate your current practices in the context of the principles covered in this Golden Star. Consider how you can utilize your developer style, initiatives, and learning practices, to establish a path for personal and professional growth.

1. **Assess your developer style** Reflect on your style of leadership and how you use it to develop others. Are you a Doctor, Expert, Coach, or Counsellor? Are there situations where you might need to adapt your preferred style to better serve your team?

2. **Talent development** How do you nurture talent within your team? Do you provide opportunities for growth through mentoring and coaching? Do you use delegation as a tool for enhancing skills and building individual competence?

3. **Become a multiplier** Reflect on your ability to amplify the capabilities of your team. Is there anything you could do to make your team members feel more valued and respected? Can you find new ways to encourage open communication and bigger thinking?

After reflecting on these points, identify areas that require improvement, and set SMART goals for each one. For example: "Over the next six weeks, I will adopt the multiplier approach by organizing fortnightly brainstorming sessions aimed at amplifying the collective intelligence of my team. I will do this by encouraging each team member to contribute at least one idea or solution to a current project or challenge we are facing." As you prepare your goals, remember that as a leader, you have the capacity to drive change and foster success, both for yourself and for your team.

Endnotes

1   Lee, W., & Seo, M. G. (2021). Neural correlates of feedback processing in decision-making under risk. *Frontiers in Neuroscience*, 15, 625875. https://doi.org/10.3389/fnins.2021.625875
    Tang, Y. Y., Hölzel, B. K., & Posner, M. I. (2022). The neuroscience of mindfulness meditation. *Nature Reviews Neuroscience*, 23(4), 251-263. https://doi.org/10.1038/s41583-022-00550-5

2   Zak, P. J. (2011). Trust, morality, and oxytocin? *Science*, 322(5903), 931-932.

3   Iacoboni, M. (2009). Imitation, empathy, and mirror neurons. *Annual Review of Psychology*, 60, 653-670.

4   Doidge, N. (2007). *The brain that changes itself.* Viking.

5   Dweck, C. (2006). *Mindset: The new psychology of success.* Random House.

6   Hattie, J., & Timperley, H. (2007). The power of feedback. *Review of Educational Research*, 77(1), 81-112.

BONUS STAR
PUBLIC SPEAKING

Public speaking: Stepping into the spotlight

Public speaking is about connecting with your audience. Mastering it requires confidence, empathy, authenticity, and wit. When you give a speech, you need to be aware of not just *what* you say, but *how* you say it, *why* you say it, and *when* you say it. Authenticity is a powerful bridge between speaker and audience. When knowledge meets charisma, it sparks connections and inspires transformation.

Most of us have experienced the heart-pounding anxiety of having to address a group, all eyes focused on us. Overcoming your anxiety about speaking in public isn't about denying fear, but harnessing it. Preparation is key, so knowing your material thoroughly builds confidence. Regular practice, positive visualization, and mindfulness techniques can help you manage nervousness and instill confidence. Remember, an adrenaline rush can drive energy into your speech. As Dale Carnegie said, "Only the prepared speaker deserves to be confident".

The first step is to know your audience. Before you can decide what impact you want to make, you need to know who you are talking to, what they care about, and what resonates with them. This requires empathy, observation, and usually, some research. Once you understand your audience, you can tailor your message to hold their interest, meet their needs, and maximize your impact. A one-size-fits-all approach never works in public speaking.

Now, consider your presence on stage. An authentic presence is about being real, letting your personality shine through, and connecting with the audience. Embrace your unique style, share anecdotes, and remember that vulnerability can often add a layer of genuineness to your presentation.

Your voice, not just your words, is a powerful tool. Harness this power by using changes in pitch, tone, volume, and rate to emphasize key points and keep the audience engaged. Clear pronunciation and articulate speech will further enhance comprehension and increase the impact of your message.

Non-verbal communication, or body language, can reinforce your message, or sabotage it. Align non-verbal cues with your spoken words. From eye contact and and an open posture to using purposeful gestures and engaging facial expressions, well-tuned body language can turn your speech into a lively conversation rather than a dull monologue.

Using visual aids can help your audience understand complex concepts, focus on key points, and retain more information. These could be slides, videos, props or handouts, but whatever you choose, make sure visual aids enhance your presentation, and don't eclipse it. Keep things clear, simple, and relevant.

Captivating openings seize the audience's attention. Memorable closings leave a lasting impression. Start with a hook, such as a compelling story, surprising fact, or provocative question, and end with a powerful call to action. As the saying goes, "Well begun is half done". An impactful ending is the ribbon that neatly ties up your speech.

Add humor to keep your audience engaged. Wit can make you more relatable, but remember, humor is like salt in a recipe; a pinch can enhance the flavor, too much can ruin it.

Engaging directly with your audience through Q&A sessions provides opportunities for clarification, elaboration, and even feedback. During interactive sessions, remember to listen actively, respond thoughtfully, and respect all viewpoints.

Time your speeches carefully. Follow your prepared outline, stick to your key points, and avoid getting sidetracked. Delivering a well-structured, concise presentation is a mark of respect for your audience's time.

Be adaptable. You may need to tweak your approach to different situations. Addressing conference delegates in an auditorium is not the same as hosting a team meeting in person or online. Virtual meetings might need more engagement in the form of online chats or polls, while engaging a small group, face-to-face, presents opportunities for informal interaction.

Persuasive speech can influence thoughts, and inspire action. The power of persuasion is encapsulated in techniques, such as logical reasoning, building credibility, understanding the audience's perspective, and appealing to their emotions. Use probing questions to stimulate critical thinking, challenge assumptions, arrive at a consensus, or inspire action.

Expect the unexpected. As a speaker, you are sure to encounter technical issues, audience interruptions, and challenging questions at some point. The key here is grace under pressure. Maintain your calm, think on your feet and, if necessary, use a dash of humor to lighten the mood and regain control of the situation.

Public speaking is a powerful tool in a leader's arsenal, but it can be intimidating. However, it is a skill that can be improved through practice and rehearsal. Use NLP anchoring techniques to develop strategies for dealing with "speaker nerves". Record yourself, seek feedback from other speakers, and persistently refine your ability. With practice, you will develop an authentic presence, and become comfortable with your body language. You will learn how to make the most of visual aids, craft compelling openings and closings, handle questions deftly, adapt to different settings, and understand your audience. Mastering public speaking will give you the means to share visions, motivate teams, and drive organizational growth.

SPARK public speaking model

The SPARK model is designed to help speakers prepare for an event. It focuses on audience analysis, detailed preparation, authenticity, rehearsal, and anticipating possible challenges. Adopting this comprehensive approach will help you deliver effective, engaging, and confident presentations.

S – Study the setting and audience

- Determine the size, demographics, and nature of your audience.
- Understand the context, format, and setting of the event.
- Analyze the audience's level of knowledge about the topic.

P – Prepare and practice

- Develop key messages or takeaways for the audience.
- Structure your speech with an engaging opening, informative body, and impactful conclusion.
- Prepare visual aids that add value and clarity to your message.
- Practice your speech to improve your fluency, tone, pace, and body language.
- Record your practice sessions for self-feedback.

A – Authenticity and adaptability

- Find personal stories or experiences to illustrate key points.
- Show vulnerability where it is meaningful and authentic.
- Adapt your speech based on audience reaction, or unexpected changes.

R – Rehearse and review

- Rehearse in conditions as close as possible to the real event.
- Seek feedback from trusted individuals.
- Review and refine your speech based on feedback.

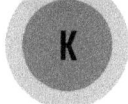

K – Know your Plan B

- Have contingency plans for potential challenges (technical issues, unexpected questions).
- Develop effective strategies to handle speaker nerves or unexpected interruptions.

SPARK PUBLIC SPEAKING MODEL

S

SETTING AND AUDIENCE STUDY
- Determine the size, demographics, and preferences of your audience.
- Understand the context, format, and setting of the event.
- Analyze the audience's knowledge level about the topic.

P

PREPARATION AND PRACTICE
- Develop and structure your speech.
- Prepare visual aids, which add value and clarity to your message.
- Practice your speech, and record and review for self-feedback.

A

AUTHENTICITY AND ADAPTABILITY
- Find personal stories or experiences to illustrate key points.
- Show vulnerability where it's meaningful and authentic.
- Adapt your speech based on the audience's reactions or event's dynamics.

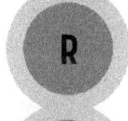

R

REHEARSAL AND REVIEW
- Rehearse your speech in conditions as close as possible to the real event.
- Seek feedback from trusted individuals.
- Review and refine your speech based on feedback.

K

KNOW YOUR "PLAN B"
- Anticipate potential challenges and have contingency plans.
- Develop strategies to handle nervousness or unexpected interruptions.

BONUS STAR
STORYTELLING

Harnessing the power of storytelling

Storytelling transforms words into vivid landscapes, brings characters to life, and weaves messages into engaging narratives. Integrating storytelling into presentations and speeches can turn them into experiences. From conducting a team meeting to delivering a keynote speech or communicating a change initiative, a well-crafted story engages your audience, drives home your points, and aligns listeners with your vision.

Good stories go beyond the simple sharing of ideas; they enter the realm of emotional connectivity. Well-crafted, genuinely told stories stir emotions, inspire action, shape perceptions, and foster a shared sense of purpose. Storytelling is a fascinating interplay between neuroscience and the human experience. Stories don't just engage our brains at the cognitive level; they also trigger emotional responses, enhancing memorability and impact. Activating areas of the brain, such as the sensory cortex, enables listeners to *experience* the story, not just hear it.

The art of storytelling revolves around the audience, and different audiences require different narratives. Effective storytelling is about adapting to the moment, to the audience, the environment, and the desired outcome. You might need to inspire your team today, but tomorrow you could be negotiating a deal, or addressing a large conference. The ability to mold your story to fit each context can significantly enhance its impact.

Crafting a story starts with establishing your core message or vision. This represents what you want to convey. It should be authentic, and resonate with your audience. Depending on the purpose, it may also motivate.

Constructing a narrative means bringing together elements such as plot, character, conflict, and resolution, in a way that captures the audience's imagination. Understanding your audience's needs, motivations and values is the key to crafting a compelling narrative. Effective stories build an emotional bridge between the teller and the listener, establishing a rapport that outlasts the narrative itself.

As leaders, our stories can inspire, motivate, and transform. They create connections, build trust, and foster a shared vision. In leadership storytelling, our narratives have the potential to shape perceptions, influence decisions, and drive change.

Key elements of storytelling

- **Structure** How you structure your story can mean the difference between a forgettable narrative and a compelling tale. The path from the introduction, through the conflict, to the resolution and conclusion, needs to be carefully laid out. Every twist and turn should keep your audience engaged, and invested in the outcome.
- **Characters and plot** These turn stories into immersive experiences. Characters represent values and struggles, whereas the plot creates a coherent, engaging narrative. From an individual's relentless pursuit of excellence to the team's success on a challenging project, memorable characters and a relatable plot give stories impact.

- **Metaphors and analogies** When used skillfully, these can turn complex ideas into relatable concepts. They act as bridges, connecting the known to the unknown, and providing new perspectives. Whether you are explaining a challenging strategy or highlighting the importance of team collaboration, metaphors and analogies can help get your message across.
- **Visual aids** Storyboards and visual aids help your audience 'see' the narrative. These aids can range from a simple sketch to a comprehensive diagram or powerful photograph. When used well, visual aids give your stories impact, and make them memorable.
- **Authenticity** Our unique experiences, struggles, and triumphs bring authenticity to our stories. Personal anecdotes provide an opportunity to share values and insights. When delivered with conviction, they resonate deeply with the audience, establishing trust and strengthening bonds.
- **Truth** Along with authenticity, truthfulness is a cornerstone of good leadership. As leaders, it is our responsibility to ensure that our stories reflect our true values and genuine experiences. Misrepresentation is not only unethical, it harms credibility and can erode trust and goodwill.
- **Success** Stories of success and resilience have the power to inspire and motivate. They embody the triumph of the human spirit, demonstrating what is possible when we push beyond our limitations. Sharing these stories can motivate others, encourage them to persevere, or persuade them to take risks in pursuit of their own goals or ambitions.
- **Cultural sensitivity** In our interconnected world, cross-cultural communication is an essential leadership skill. Adapting stories for diverse audiences involves more than just a few adjustments to language and content; it requires understanding and respecting cultural nuances. A culturally sensitive narrative can build bridges, foster understanding, and create a more inclusive environment.
- **Practice, practice, practice** Good storytelling takes practice. Use feedback to gain insight into your strongest elements, or pinpoint weak areas. Regular rehearsals will refine your narrative, enhance delivery, and build confidence. As you discover what works and what doesn't work, you'll be able to make the most of your storytelling skills.

Storytelling framework

Use this framework to help you craft and deliver stories that inspire, engage, and motivate. For leaders, the power of storytelling lies in the ability to transform abstract ideas into relatable narratives that forge a deep connection with the audience.

Discover your story

- **Use your experiences** Draw from personal experiences and/or company history to find stories that embody the values and vision you wish to convey.
- **Unearth key messages** Identify the main themes and messages you would like your audience to take away from your story.

Develop characters and a plot

- **Characters** Create relatable characters. They could be like you, your team members, or someone else connected to your message.
- **Plot** Define the storyline or sequence of events. Remember, good plots often involve a challenge or conflict that has to be resolved.

Structure your story

- **Set the scene** Provide enough background for the audience to understand the context.
- **Conflict** Introduce a problem or challenge that must be overcome.
- **Climax** Create a peak, where the tension is highest.
- **Resolution** Present a new solution or innovative way to resolve or overcome the challenge.
- **Conclusion** Wrap up the story by highlighting the lessons learned, and ensuring the outcome is clear.

Incorporate emotional elements

- **Use emotional hooks** Connect with your audience on an emotional level through humor, surprise, suspense, or sharing relatable struggles and achievements.
- **Use sensory language** Engage your audience's senses to make your story vivid and more immersive.

Deliver with authenticity

- **Be genuine** Authenticity resonates with people. Stories that are sincere and truthful can demonstrate both your vulnerabilities and your strengths.
- **Practice your delivery** Ensure your vocal tones, gestures, body language, and facial expressions match the story's emotions.

Adapt to your audience

- **Know your audience** Understand their needs, values, and perspectives.
- **Tailor the story** Adapt the content, language, and delivery based on cultural nuances, and/or the audience's familiarity with the context.

Rehearse and refine

- **Practice** Rehearse your story multiple times to enhance your delivery.
- **Seek feedback** Honest comments from trusted individuals will help you refine your storytelling skills.

Use visual aids and metaphors

- **Visual aids** If relevant, use photographs, diagrams, or props to enhance your story.
- **Metaphors** Use metaphors and analogies to make complex ideas more relatable and understandable.

EPILOGUE

I hope you have found much in these pages to inspire and encourage you, and that the insights revealed by the Golden Stars will become a catalyst for meaningful change in your leadership practice.

Together, we've explored what it means to be an effective leader, but leadership isn't just about knowledge; it's about action, and embodying the principles of purpose-driven leadership every single day.

I look forward to this being the start of an ongoing conversation about your leadership development, a springboard to greater heights on your journey. Connect with me on social media for vibrant conversations about leadership, and join our community of leaders across the globe. Check out my website for resources and opportunities to engage in discussions that will enhance your leadership skills. Also consider the **10 Golden Stars to Leadership Excellence Masterclass** (page 262) for opportunities to interact with fellow leaders, and receive personalized coaching that will help you unlock your leadership potential. And, if you are ready to take the next step on your journey, consider one-on-one coaching sessions with me (page 263). Together, we'll tailor a plan to meet your needs.

As you continue to grow and develop, remember that your actions have the power to inspire others and transform your business. Lead with purpose, learn with passion, and together, let's shape a legacy of excellence.

Thank you for your commitment to growth. Until we meet again, may your leadership journey be filled with powerful insights, positive experiences, and long-lasting impact.

Tom Dreyer

www.drtomdreyer.com

MASTERCLASS

Your journey doesn't end here. For those inspired to delve deeper and apply these principles in a dynamic, interactive setting, we invite you to an extension of this enlightening experience: the **10 Golden Stars to Leadership Excellence Masterclass**.

Designed to complement the insights and wisdom found in this book, this masterclass series is your opportunity to engage with the insights on a new level. Through a blend of practical tools, neuroscientific strategies, and real-world applications, each episode is crafted to help you navigate the complexities of modern leadership, turning obstacles into remarkable growth opportunities.

Bonus features:
✓ Application of advanced toolkits
✓ Engaging stories and case studies
✓ Expert-led sessions by the author of this book
✓ Deep self-reflection opportunities
✓ Fast-track ticket for 1-on-1 coaching with Dr. Tom Dreyer
✓ Access to leadership networking community

Each episode promises to be a transformative experience, offering a richer, more practical approach to mastering the art of leadership. Whether you aspire to inspire, lead teams more effectively, or navigate the evolving landscape of leadership in the 21st century, this masterclass is an invaluable next step.

Enroll now
drtomdreyer.com/masterclass

COACHING

Join Dr. Dreyer for a transformative coaching opportunity

This book has equipped you with foundational knowledge and insights, but true mastery comes from translating knowledge into action.

Our coaching journey will offer you:

- **Enhanced self-awareness**: Transform your preferred leadership style and growth opportunities into a personal superpower.
- **Improved communication skills**: Convey your vision and values effectively to motivate and inspire your teams, peers, and executives.
- **Boosted emotional intelligence**: Apply EQ and NLP to manage your emotions and those of others to foster a collaborative environment.
- **Career advancement**: Strategically position yourself for better opportunities with a targeted development agenda.

Who is it for?

- **Executives** seeking to enhance interpersonal skills, strategic decision-making, and organizational influence.
- **High-potentials** for an accelerated development journey.
- **Groups** to enhance collective capabilities and achieve shared objectives.
- **Specialized needs,** such as career transitions, behavioral change, productivity, engagement, and more.

We will tailor a coaching program that suits your unique needs and sets you on a path to excellence. Interested? Reach us at drtomdreyer.com/coaching/ or leadership@drtomdreyer.com

REFERENCES

Anderson, Lorin W., & David R. Krathwohl, eds. (2001). *A Taxonomy for Learning, Teaching, and Assessing: A Revision of Bloom's Taxonomy of Educational Objectives.* (Rev. ed.) Addison-Wesley Longman, Inc.

Bandler, R., & Grinder, J. (1975). *The Structure of Magic, Vol. I: A Book about Language and Therapy.* Science and Behavior Books.

Bar-On, R., & Parker, J. D. A. (2000). *The Handbook of Emotional Intelligence.* Jossey-Bass.

Bartz, J. A., Zaki, J., Bolger, N., & Ochsner, K. N. (2011). Social Effects of Oxytocin in Humans: Context and Person Matter. *Trends in Cognitive Sciences,* 15(7), 301-309.

Baumgartner, T., Heinrichs, M., Vonlanthen, A., Fischbacher, U., & Fehr, E. (2008). Oxytocin Shapes the Neural Circuitry of Trust and Trust Adaptation in Humans. *Neuron,* 58(4), 639-650.

Belbin, R. M. (2010). *Management Teams: Why They Succeed or Fail.* (3rd ed.) Taylor & Francis.

Brownell, J. (2023). *Listening: Attitudes, Principles, and Skills.* (7th ed.) Routledge.

Carnegie, D. (1998). *How to Win Friends and Influence People.* (Rev. ed.) Simon & Schuster.

Carnegie, D., & Associates (2012). *How to Win Friends and Influence People in the Digital Age.* Simon & Schuster.

Csikszentmihalyi, M. (2008). *Flow: The Psychology of Optimal Experience.* (Rev. ed.) Harper Perennial Modern Classics.

Covey, S. M. R. (2006). *The Speed of Trust: The One Thing That Changes Everything.* Free Press.

Covey, S. R. (2020). *The 7 Habits of Highly Effective People.* (30th Anniversary Edition.) Simon and Schuster.

De Dreu, C. K. W. (2012). Oxytocin Modulates Cooperation Within and Competition Between Groups: An Integrative Review and Research Agenda. *Hormones and Behavior,* 61(3), 419-428.

Dweck, C. S. (2006). *Mindset: The New Psychology of Success.* Random House.

Feltman, C. (2009). *The Thin Book of Trust: An Essential Primer for Building Trust at Work.* Thin Book Publishing.

Goleman, D. (2020). *Emotional Intelligence: Why It Can Matter More than IQ.* (25th Anniversary Edition.) Bloomsbury Publishing.

Green, C. H., Galford, R. M., & Maister, D. H. (2000). *The Trusted Advisor.* Free Press.

Hersey, P., Blanchard, K. H., & Johnson, D. E. (2012). *Management of Organizational Behavior: Leading Human Resources.* (10th ed.) Pearson.

Hiatt, J. (2006). *ADKAR: A Model for Change in Business, Government and our Community.* Prosci Learning Center Publications.

Kosfeld, M., Heinrichs, M., Zak, P. J., Fischbacher, U., & Fehr, E. (2005). Oxytocin Increases Trust in Humans. *Nature*, 435(7042), 673-676.

Kotter, J. P. (2012). *Leading Change.* (Rev. ed.) Harvard Business Review Press.

Kouzes, J. M., & Posner, B. Z. (2023). *The Leadership Challenge: How to Make Extraordinary Things Happen in Organizations.* (7th ed.) Jossey-Bass.

Madsen, S. (2019). *The Power of Project Leadership: 7 Keys to help you transform from project manager to project leader.* Kogan Page Limited.

Maister, D., Green, C., & Galford, R. (2000). *The Trusted Advisor.* Free Press.

Marston, W. M. (2014). *Emotions of Normal People.* (Rev. ed.) Read & Co., Science.

Maslow, A. H. (2017). *A Theory of Human Motivation.* (Rev. ed.) www.bnpublishing.com

Maxwell, J. C. (2011). *The 5 Levels of Leadership.* Center Street.

Myers, I. B., & Myers, P. B. (1980). *Gifts Differing: Understanding Personality Type.* Davies-Black Publishing.

Palmer, H. (1988). *The Enneagram: Understanding Yourself and the Others in Your Life.* Harper & Row.

Pink, D. H. (2009). *Drive: The Surprising Truth About What Motivates Us.* Riverhead Books.

Royal, M., & Porath, C. (2004). *The Engagement Imperative.* Harvard Business Review Press.

Salovey, P., & Mayer, J. D. (1990). Emotional Intelligence. Imagination, Cognition and Personality. *Sage Journals*, 9(3), 185-211.

Serrat, O. (2017). *The Five Whys Technique. In: Knowledge Solutions: Tools, Methods and Approaches to Drive Organizational Performance.* Springer Singapore.

Shamay-Tsoory, S. G., & Abu-Akel, A. (2016). The Social Salience Hypothesis of Oxytocin. *Biological Psychiatry*, 79(3), 194-202.

Tuckman, B. W. (1965). Developmental Sequence in Small Groups. *Psychological Bulletin*, 63(6), 384-399.

Whitmore, J., & Performance Consultants International. (2017). *The Grow Model. In: Coaching for Performance: The Principles and Practice of Coaching for Leadership.* (5th ed.) Nicholas Brealey.

Wiseman, L. (2010). *Multipliers: How the Best Leaders Make Everyone Smarter.* HarperBusiness.

Zak, P. J., Kurzban, R., & Matzner, W. T. (2005). Oxytocin is Associated with Human Trustworthiness. *Hormones and Behavior*, 48(5), 522-527.

INDEX

ABOUT THE AUTHOR

Dr. Tom Dreyer's distinguished career of 20+ years has been defined by a commitment to excellence and a dedication to empowering leaders globally. From humble beginnings in South Africa to becoming a respected leadership authority, his story reflects immense passion and determination for transformative change.

At 14, living independently, Tom managed school, work, and entrepreneurial endeavors, cultivating a robust work ethic and commitment to personal growth. His professional path began at SASOL, where he advanced from being an operator to becoming the principal of learning and development.

In 2014, a relocation to Abu Dhabi marked a significant expansion in his global influence. At ADNOC and beyond, he led the design, development, and deployment of award-winning leadership programs in partnership with prestigious institutions such as Harvard, London Business School, FranklinCovey, and many more. He has developed over 4000 leaders from 119 nationalities, serving as program director and subject matter expert.

Tom holds a master's degree in human resources management and a doctorate in talent development, with his academic endeavors rooted in neuroscience, enhancing his leadership development approach.

Recognized with numerous accolades, including a PRISM award and a CIPD award for Best Learning & Development Program, Tom is also a credentialed coach with the International Coaching Federation and a member of the British Psychology Society.

Beyond the corporate setting, Tom contributes to academia as a university faculty lecturer, moderator, and board member. His interests include scuba diving, exploring new cultures and human behaviors through travel, reading, delivering key notes, and coaching that reflects his lifelong learning philosophy.

At home, Tom cherishes time with his loving wife and two boys. He serves as a philanthropist by giving back to youth in need, believing that today's children are tomorrow's leaders.

10 Golden Stars to Leadership Excellence captures Tom Dreyer's mission to equip leaders with vital tools and insights for effective, empathetic, and transformative leadership. His work inspires leaders to pursue excellence with purpose and passion, setting the foundation for a lasting legacy.